ALLAGASH

MAINE'S WILD AND SCENIC RIVER

ALLAGASH

MAINE'S WILD AND SCENIC RIVER

Dean Bennett

*with Photographs and Illustrations
by the Author*

Down East Books

To Sheila,
and
to those who preserved and continue to protect
the Allagash Wilderness Waterway

Down East Books
P.O. Box 679, Camden, Maine 04843

Bennett, Dean B.
   Allagash: Maine's wild and scenic river / Dean Bennett.
with photographs and illustrations by the author.
      p.   cm.
   Includes bibliographical references (p.) and index.
   ISBN 0-89272-332-7 (hardcover)
   1. Allagash River (Me.) 2. Natural History—Maine—Allagash
River. I. Title
   F27.A4B46 1994
   974.1'1—dc20   94-14451
                                                          CIP

Contents

Preface

Allagash! The word alone, in the minds of many, conjures up images of a remote, uninhabited wilderness to the north. And for good reason: the Allagash River and its headwaters in northern Maine flow for a hundred miles through an isolated, forested region where dense stands of spruce, fir, and northern hardwoods line the river and overhang its brooks and streams, where the shores of its lakes and ponds appear largely undisturbed, and where views of the surrounding hills and mountains show an expanse of forested land. So rich in natural diversity is this waterway that it captures the true essence of one of our country's great wildernesses—the north woods. "There are no hundred miles in America quite their equal," wrote the late Supreme Court justice William O. Douglas, "Certainly none has their distinctive quality."[1]

In the mid-1960s, a few years after Justice Douglas wrote so expressively and warmly of this river, the citizens of Maine approved the purchase and protection of the Allagash Wilderness Waterway. Thus they created in the midst of an increasingly domesticated world the opportunity to return to a wilder, more primitive past. Today, surrounded by land managed for its timber resource, this narrow strip of waterway still provides a sense of the northern forest of an earlier day. Here one can gain impressions reminiscent of a time when the interrelationships upon which nature depends were free to work without human intrusion.

Like a Chinese garden on a grand scale, where all forces of nature are represented and their harmony promoted, this wilderness waterway increases the natural well-being of the entire country. Visiting it or just knowing that it exists contributes to a sense of our own wholeness—a feeling that we are an integral part of the natural world. Capturing some of this feeling is, I believe, the challenge of this book.

Today the wilderness character of the north woods is diminishing. This is true even within and around the protected zone of the Allagash Wilderness Waterway, although viewed from the waters within the waterway, the changes here are often subtle and revealed best over time. It has been thirty years now since I first dipped my paddle into Telos Lake, and steadily I have become aware of the increasing presence of the internal combustion engine, the multiplying overflights, the growing number of access roads, the prevalence of sand and silt deposits at the mouths of brooks and streams, and the proximity of forest harvesting activities.

Among those areas set aside to preserve a sense of wildness, wilderness waterway corridors, in particular, pose unique and difficult challenges for those charged with their management. The vulnerability of these areas to the effects of activities both within and beyond their boundaries requires the protective interest and cooperation of many individuals and organizations from both public and private sectors. Many positive examples of such shared responsibility have been demonstrated in the Allagash Wilderness Waterway since its creation, but if its wilderness character is to be retained for future generations, there must be a continuing commitment on the part of all who use and influence it.

There are those who will say that a book such as this will encourage more people to visit the Allagash and thus further diminish the values the wilderness area was set aside to protect. However, history shows that increasing pressures on natural areas are inevitable in light of a growing, increasingly affluent and mobile population. Wilderness areas need advocates who will work to safeguard their natural values. To this end, I hope that the images presented here will convey an understanding and appreciation of this unique forest that sweeps across our country's northern border. Even more important, I hope that this book will underscore the need and urgency to identify and protect natural areas in the north woods that best represent its remote, wilderness character. The Allagash Wilderness Waterway exemplifies what we can gain by their protection.

Throughout the long but pleasant process of researching this book, I collected data from many sources. A number of experts were consulted about various aspects of the subject, books and articles were searched for pertinent information, and trips were made in all seasons to study and photograph the waterway. One canoe trip lasted twenty-two days and resulted in an extensive journal of observations and impressions as well as more than two thousand color slides. The synthesis and interpretation of the voluminous amount of information is the result of my best judgement, and I alone must take responsibility for any errors.

The production of a book such as this cannot be carried out alone. There are many individuals to whom I am indebted. First and foremost, this book would have been an impossibility without the total support and active participation of my wife, Sheila. Her insights and advice were invaluable throughout all phases of the book's development—from the initial proposal through the planning of the canoe trips, the writing of the manuscript, the creation of the illustrations, and the making of the photographs. She accompanied me on all nine trips made to the region to photograph and gather material. Together we coped with the anxieties of a blizzard, thunderstorms, high waves, and even a hurricane. But we also shared the excitement of whitewater canoeing, the thrill of wildlife encounters, and the beauty of sunsets.

I'm also especially indebted to a very special group of people who are responsible for managing the Allagash Wilderness Waterway—men and women who are dedicated to protecting the natural integrity of this wilderness area. I give special thanks to Tim Caverly, supervisor of the waterway, and

Susan Caverly, clerk with the waterway staff, whose friendship, support, and generosity not only paved the way for much of my research and fieldwork but made the book possible in innumerable ways. Tim's thorough reading of the manuscript and thoughtful comments and suggestions were especially helpful.

Jon Metcalf, the waterway ranger at Allagash Lake, and Margie Austin also played several pivotal roles, especially in the fieldwork, which included finding my lost glasses on a remote beach on Allagash Lake. For their friendship, encouragement, and many kindnesses I am grateful.

Pat Reardon, the waterway ranger stationed on Churchill Lake, generously shared his extensive knowledge of the area and assisted me in visiting a number of sites. He and his wife, Colleen, graciously shared their cabin and dinner table. I thank them both.

I also thank Jim Kelly, the waterway ranger on Chamberlain Lake, and Glenda Kelly, receptionist with the waterway staff, who provided much information, hot coffee on cold days, and warning of Hurricane Bob.

I am also appreciative of information and support from David Milligan, the waterway ranger at Michaud Farm on the lower part of the Allagash River, and Linda Milligan, receptionist with the waterway staff. With David's help I was able to time my photographic visit to Twin Brook Ledges to coincide with the blooming of the exceptional wildflowers growing there.

I am grateful for the generous help I received from Faye Hafford and her late husband, Lee, who both retired from the waterway staff during the production of this book. I was amazed at the river navigational skills of Lee, who guided us on a spring journey through rapids up the river from the town of Allagash to McKeen Brook below the falls. He will be missed in the Allagash.

I am also thankful for help from Tom Coon, the waterway ranger on Eagle Lake, who kept Churchill Dam open a little longer one day so that I could photograph Chase Rapids with the sun in the right position; Brady Scott, former waterway ranger on Eagle Lake and now retired, who gave directions to a number of locations and shared his extensive knowledge of the area; Larry Nadeau, the waterway ranger on Umsaskis Lake, who found us at the Squirrel Pocket campsite on Round Pond one day and shared his knowledge of the area; and Eric Hoar, assistant waterway ranger at Umsaskis Lake, who answered questions about that section of the river.

I am especially indebted to John Richardson and Regina Webster, who operate Nugent's Chamberlain Lake Camps. For their generosity, interest, friendship, as well as their logistical help and knowledge of the waterway, I am most grateful and extend a very special thank-you.

For their hospitality and information on the region I thank Jim Drake, dam tender at Telos Lake, and Micki McNally, owner of McNally Sporting Camps on Ross Stream. And for special transportation assistance I thank Norman L'Italien and Stanley Lazore, of Pelletier's Campground, and Eddie Raymond, of Katahdin Outfitters.

I also thank the following persons who helped answer my questions about various aspects of the natural history of the waterway and surrounding region: Robert Marvinney and Woodrow Thompson, geologists with the Maine Geological Survey; Stephen Pollock, geologist at the University of Southern Maine; Florence Grosvenor, geologist; Hank Tyler, manager of the Maine Critical Areas Program; Charlie Todd, wildlife biologist and eagle specialist with the Endangered Species Group, Maine Department of Inland Fisheries and Wildlife; Linda Welch, wildlife biologist and researcher working with eagles; Jonathan Miller and Paul Hersey, soil conservationists with the Soil Conservation Service; Ed Sturges, naturalist; Charles Cogbill, forest ecologist; Caroline Elliot, senior planner, Maine Department of Conservation; Fred Todd, Maine Lakes Study, Maine Department of Conservation; Craig Tenbroek, Maine Rivers Study, Maine Department of Conservation; and Tom Shoener, Director of Public Information and Education, Maine Department of Inland Fisheries and Wildlife.

I am also grateful to the following persons who helped locate and provide opportunities to photograph references for some of the pen-and-ink illustrations: Marilyn Dwelley, botanist; Vance Wells, professor of botany at the University of Maine at Farmington; John Mudge, retired professor of biological science at the University of Maine at Farmington; David Locke, superintendent of hatcheries, Maine Department of Inland Fisheries and Wildlife; Gerald Grant, fish culturist and supervisor, and Paul Campbell, temporary fish culturist, at the Phillips Hatchery, Maine Department of Inland Fisheries and Wildlife; Mark McCollough, director of the Maine Caribou Project; David Wilbur, superintendent of the Gray Game Farm, Maine Department of Inland Fisheries and Wildlife; Stephen Arthur, Furbearer/Bear Project, Maine Department of Inland Fisheries and Wildlife; and Mika and Heather of York's Wild Kingdom. I appreciate, too, the attention and care the people at Maine Color Service gave to the processing of my photographic images.

I also thank the following at the University of Maine at Farmington: my administrators for their support—President Michael Orenduff, Provost Sue Huseman, Acting Dean of Education Betsey Squibb, and professor Stephen Godomsky, chairman of the Middle and Secondary Education Department; the Faculty Development Committee for research support; Fred Dearnley, photographic specialist, and Stacey Hodges, graphics specialist, for their support and assistance; and Sylvia Hodgkins, administrative assistant, and Michael Leahey, technical systems coordinator, for help and advice.

Finally, I acknowledge the continued faith Down East Books has in my work and especially thank Karin Womer for her friendly encouragement and valuable advice.

—Dean Bennett, Mt. Vernon, Maine

A NOTE FOR VISITORS TO THE ALLAGASH WILDERNESS WATERWAY

This state-owned natural area, now designated as a National Wild and Scenic River, is a relatively narrow corridor flanking the Allagash waterway. Most of the land beyond five hundred feet from the high-water mark of the river, lakes, ponds, and streams is privately owned. Land within the five-hundred-foot zone is publicly owned for the purpose of protecting wilderness character and scenic natural beauty. Respecting the property rights of private landowners and the unique natural character of the waterway, including its wildlife, plants, geologic features, and cultural artifacts, is a responsibility all visitors must share.

A narrow stream bodered by tamarack winds through a developing wetland that is slowly filling in a cove. Allagash Mountain rises in the distance.

The Allagash

Downwind, three miles away, it sounds like a background whisper—a quiet hiss in the forest. But at its edge, Allagash Falls churns and roars, controlled only by the chance configuration of its outcropping. Ruffled curtains, frothy and white, drape the rocks, half concealing the river's sculpting of the purple-black slate. These dark sheets of stone once lay level until forces immeasurably larger than that of flowing water thrust them nearly vertical. Now the river exploits weaknesses between the layers of upturned rock as it plunges through two eroded chutes to converge in a deep pool thirty feet below. Here it swirls disorientedly, recovers, and escapes from the confining dark rock walls.

The power of flowing water is channeled by the land to produce a dramatic symbol of Maine's wild and scenic river— Allagash Falls.

A waterfall is the result of a marriage of land and water, a chance union that produces a unique attribute of a river's personality. Humans are drawn to a waterfall by its beauty and power, its ability to touch all the senses, and by a kind of stability it imparts to nature. It seems ageless, a remnant of a wilderness past. Its presence is dependable, and its character appears unchanging. But a waterfall is only seemingly so, for a river, such as that which passes through those chutes at Allagash Falls, is never exactly the same, its waters contain the history of the entire river above. Every arriving molecule of the Allagash River, if it were able, would relate a different story of the journey from the river's headwaters: perhaps of trickling from beneath moss-covered boulders along densely wooded shores or sluicing through gorges and over falls of 400-million-year-old slate, perhaps of being pushed by strong winds and violently hurled against shores of volcanic rock or of gently washing ancient reefs of fossilized coral; or maybe the river's tale would tell of being jostled by moose or eagles plying inlets and coves or being detained in ponds engineered by beavers, or maybe of confinement within the cool, expanding cells of sphagnum—the prevalent moss of bogs and swamps.

Collectively these events, as minute and subtle as they might seem, become the mood of the river, for a river is not a separate entity: it is a reflection of its

environment. It is the pulse of the land—a vibrant connecting nerve that brings life to its watershed. Every moment and event, wherever it occurs in that watershed, is recorded in the river's flow. And here along the Allagash Wilderness Waterway, as in other areas of the north woods where nature is allowed to proceed relatively undisturbed, there is much to record.

Among wild rivers, few can match the natural diversity of the Allagash. Its headwaters, remote and picturesque, rise among hills and mountains of volcanic rock that cast their shadows during the final light of day over the "jewel" of the waterway, Allagash Lake. Below the lake a narrow, intimate stream flows eastward, in some places deep, quiet, and slow and in others shallow, noisy, and quick. At its mouth lies an expansive system of lakes, sheets of water miles long in every direction with spectacular views of Maine's highest mountain, Katahdin. The lakes drain northward to the river, where they burst forth, releasing their pent-up energy in a fury of whitewater. Swelled by surges of water from its tributaries, the river continues, alternately quiet and slow-moving through lakes and ponds, then sibilantly brisk over reappearing slaty gray ledges. Reaching the St. John River, the water is still clear and fast, retaining the spirit it exhibited in its distant headwaters. This is the Allagash—an invitation to explore the north woods.

A vast forest of spruce and fir sweeps across the upper latitudes of North America. Along its southern edge in northern areas of New England and New York, red spruce tends to replace the more northerly white spruce as the dominant companion to balsam fir. Here, too, the northern hardwoods are major components of the forest. For a hundred miles, the Allagash Wilderness Waterway flows through this forest, providing a unique opportunity to explore the rich natural diversity of the north woods.

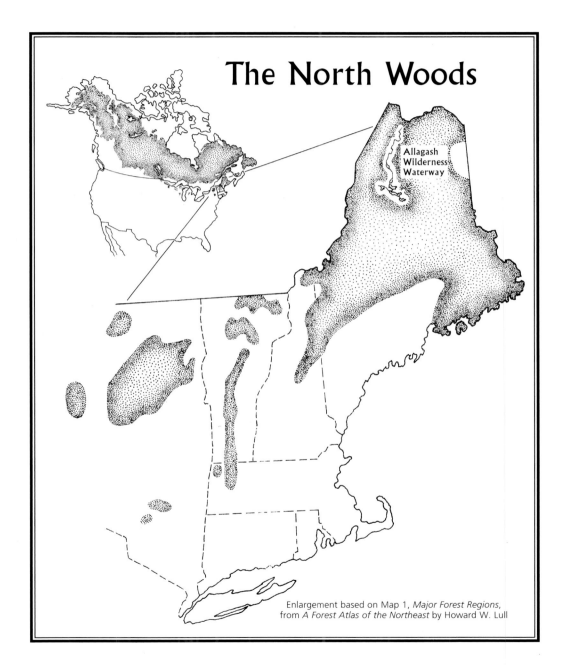

The North Woods

Allagash
Wilderness
Waterway

Enlargement based on Map 1, *Major Forest Regions*, from *A Forest Atlas of the Northeast* by Howard W. Lull

The Headwaters

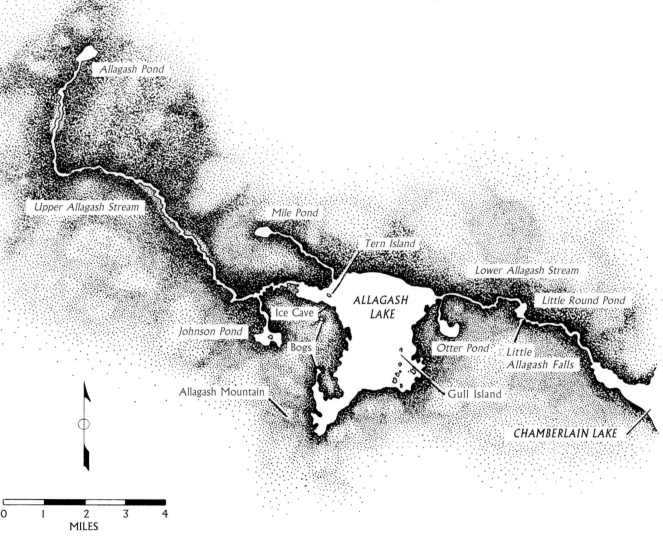

Allagash Pond

Upper Allagash Stream

Mile Pond

Tern Island

Lower Allagash Stream

ALLAGASH LAKE

Little Round Pond

Ice Cave

Johnson Pond

Bogs

Otter Pond

Little Allagash Falls

Allagash Mountain

Gull Island

CHAMBERLAIN LAKE

0 1 2 3 4
MILES

Something unusual happened here! It's immediately apparent in the chain of mountains skirting the west shore of Allagash Lake. Unlike the lower, rolling hills that define much of the region's topography, these mountains are rough, steep, and nubbly. Sharp ledges rend the ragged coat of evergreens and hardwoods clinging to the steep slopes, hinting of a violent past. Now calm prevails and a deep silence—so silent sometimes that even breathing impinges on the stillness. Few today know this gift of quiet from undisturbed expanses of the north woods, but the Wabanakis did. It was part of the lives of these Native Americans, a baseline from which sounds crucial to their survival could be singled out—an approaching wind, a waterfall around a turn in the river, the rustle of an animal in the forest.

The Indians gave this place its name. Allagaskwigamook, "Bark Cabin Lake," they called the lake below the mountains. Today it's known as Allagash Lake and shares its name with one of the mountains shaping its western shoreline. From the lake it's this mountain that first catches the eye, rising some eight hundred feet above the water. Only on the big lakes below does the relief again capture such interest. By its height and placement, Allagash Mountain's summit promises to reveal much about the land beyond the densely wooded shores of these headwaters.

THE MOUNTAIN

One of the first discoveries on the summit of Allagash Mountain is the difference between the steep easterly face it presents to the lake and its western side. The "back" of the mountain descends gradually to the valley below; in fact, a great many of the surrounding hills and mountains display an amazingly similar skewed profile—steep slopes and ledges facing slightly south of east and longer, lower slopes to the northwest. What could account for this pattern? The answer is found

in events thousands of years in the past—events that changed and shaped the character of the north woods more than any in recent time. And the clues that enabled geologists to piece together in tentative detail this region's fascinating history are found along the entire length of the waterway.

A monstrous plate of ice was responsible for the most recent major alteration of the mountain and the surface features throughout these northern areas.[1] The Laurentide Ice Sheet, as it is called, formed over Canada twenty-five thousand years ago as a result of climatic cooling. The buildup of snow to colossal depths caused enormous pressure, transforming the mass into ice and initiating a slow, ominously creeping movement outward from its domed center.

The first flow to scrape and gouge its way across Maine is believed to have had its source near present-day Quebec City. On an east-southeast course, it overtopped Allagash Mountain sometime well before twenty-one thousand years ago, by which time it had completely covered Maine and crept out onto the continental shelf. The ice sheet grew in thickness to more than three times the height of Allagash Mountain. With its tremendous weight and accumulated debris of fractured, pulverized rock, the moving ice bulldozed its way across the landscape. Encountering the resistant bedrock of hills and mountains, the glacier inched up and over them, grinding their northwesterly slopes into smooth, rounded ramps. Once over their tops, the ice mass slumped down and plucked away their fractured southeastern faces, often leaving steep, jagged cliffs in its wake. Thus the mountains and hills were left streamlined and molded, reflecting the direction of the glacier's flow.

Despite its rugged appearance when viewed from afar, the exposed rock at the top of Allagash Mountain is surprisingly smooth. A close inspection, however, corroborates one's first impression of the mountain's violent history. Beneath its weathered, pinkish surface, the rock is dark, tight-grained volcanic basalt. Recent fractures show the presence of beautiful "frozen" fragments of the greenish mineral epidote intermingled with small chunks of earthy red iron ore. It is thought that this rock bubbled up over 400 million years ago when the mountain was part of a coastline at the edge of a sea. Comparatively, the glacier was a "yesterday" occurrence and made but a superficial change on the landscape.

The top of the mountain is today almost as barren as the glacier left it. Soils are thin or completely absent, and those plants able to gain a foothold live a tenuous life exposed to the elements. The scattered, surviving trees often appear as flags, their scraggly limbs pointing away from the prevailing westerly winds in the direction taken by that ancient sheet of ice.

A SENSE OF UNITY

From Allagash Mountain one can see almost the entire waterway, stretching northerly until it blurs with the sky. These New England uplands look low and flat from this height but in reality are hilly and rolling. In effect, the land's undulating surface verifies much of what the mountain says about the rock and the forces working on it: where rocks are hard and resistant the land is high, and where they are weak the land is low. It is clear that bedrock controls the land's fundamental shape and form and defines the boundaries of the watershed.

Measured from its extreme southern boundary to its northern rendezvous with the St. John, the Allagash watershed spans sixty miles. From east to west, it is over thirty miles wide. Thus, the Allagash River funnels the drainage from 1,650 square miles of land, some of the water starting nearly a quarter of a mile high, from the tops of the watershed's remote highlands.[2] One suspects that in spite of its relatively low elevation Allagash Mountain must be visible from vantage points throughout the waterway—and, in fact, it is, creating a rare sense of unity between the watershed's headwaters, lakes, and river.

To the west of the mountain, as far as the eye can see, a vast, remote wood-

Silhouetted by a setting sun, Allagash Mountain, thirteen miles distant, dramatically extends its presence to the waters of Chamberlain Lake.

land conceals much of the landscape's tumultuous past. One can imagine that somewhere not far away on this western side there exists a single tree whose branches direct the water from every rainstorm into three different watersheds. Indeed, there is in this remote corner of northern Maine one conceivable starting point where the drainages of three rivers conjoin—the Penobscot, the upper St. John, and the Allagash. If this point lies in a still-undisturbed tract of spruce-fir woodland, it would be nearly impossible to find. So impenetrable is this kind of forest that Thoreau was moved to write that "there is hardly room for the smoke to go up."[3]

THE CONTROL OF CLIMATE

This is the forest of northern lands—a forest where climate is a powerful determinant of which kinds of trees will survive. The Allagash is in one of the coldest areas in the northeastern United States. Surprisingly, this is not entirely due to the region's northerly position on the globe; other areas at this latitude of between forty-six and forty-seven degrees are warmer. Weather patterns are responsible for the lower temperature. By a twist of meteorological fate, this northeastern section of the country is the funnel end of low-pressure weather systems that sweep across New England on an average of twice a week. Their circulation pattern tends to draw down cold air from Canadian high-pressure systems. The result: annual temperature averages less than forty degrees Fahrenheit in the Allagash region—about four degrees cooler than in central Maine.

Forty to sixty days of the year experience subzero readings. Daily temperatures in winter average only about twenty degrees Fahrenheit.

It is also a wet region, with close to forty inches of precipitation per year. Together, the cold and moisture produce an average of ten feet of snow annually. Cold temperatures keep the white cover on the ground throughout the entire winter season, leaving a growing time of only 100 to 120 days. The cool climate also holds evaporation in check, thus more moisture is available for the forest. The cold also slows the rate of decay and the release of valuable nitrogen into soils

From Allagash Mountain one can see Allagash Lake, and beyond, to the north, almost the entire Allagash watershed.

that already tend to have their nutrients "locked up" because of their highly acid nature.

THE NORTH WOODS

Cold Canadian air drawn southward by the weather patterns crossing the region exerts a powerful influence on the Allagash forest. Spruce and fir thrive in the cool temperatures, but so do the northern hardwoods, for the region lies in a transition zone between the true boreal forest to the north and the temperate deciduous forest to the south. Here, red spruce (*Picea rubens*) tends to replace the more northerly

white spruce (*Picea glauca*) as a companion to balsam fir (*Abies balsamea*). Their coniferous associates include northern white cedar (*Thuja occidentalis*), tamarack (*Larix larichina*), eastern hemlock (*Tsuga canadensis*), black spruce (*Picea mariana*), white spruce, eastern white pine (*Pinus strobus*), and occasionally red pine (*Pinus resinosa*). Among the northern hardwoods, paper birch (*Betula papyrifera*) is another close associate of these conifers, creating bright patches in the forest.

Each species has its preferred place. In the swamps northern white cedar dominates. Where drier, warmer upland conditions exist, patches of the northern hardwood forest take over. These are often dominated by sugar maple (*Acer saccharum*), American beech (*Fagus grandifolia*), and yellow birch (*Betula alleghaniensis*). But in the colder bottomlands, where saturated soils are slow to release their nutrients, and on the cool northern slopes, only the conifers can successfully compete.

Spruce and fir are especially well adapted to the cold, wet, snowy conditions of the north woods. Their cone-shaped forms and supple branches allow them to shrug off the accumulating snow. When the deep freeze of winter is in the offing, chemical and physical changes in the cells of the conifers enable them to withstand winter temperatures of minus-eighty degrees Fahrenheit or even lower.

Where the spruce-fir design really comes to the fore is in the canopy—the center of food production. Unlike their deciduous relatives, whose leaves freeze and drop off, these conifers retain their needlelike leaves. Thick clusters of short, narrow needles—millions on a single tree—break up wind flow, reducing wind chill and evaporation as well as minimizing heat loss to circulating convection currents. Only a small portion of each needle's surface is exposed to the elements. A thick outer layer further protects the needle from freezing and drying. Stomata openings for the exchange of gases are sunk deeply into its protected lower surface. When the temperature drops too low, the leaves shut down and lie dormant, ready to start photosynthesis quickly when spring thawing occurs. And since these conifers don't shed their needles as often as the deciduous trees, less new growth is required and less energy is consumed. All of these features enable them to conduct their photosynthetic food-making activities for a greater part of the year.

PHANTOM OF THE FOREST

Animals of this northern forest also have their methods for surviving the cold and snow, and they exhibit a variety of strategies. Many animals, such as warblers and ducks, leave the region in winter for warmer climates, while others—for example, black bear (*Ursus americanus*) and the American toad (*Bufo americanus*)—become inactive, slowly meting out energy reserves while overwintering in protective dens and nooks. Some, including the spruce grouse (*Dendragapus canadensis*), moose (*Alces alces*), and coyote (*Canis latrans*), are well suited for active, year-round living. Among the larger mammals, the lynx (*Felis lynx*) is one that exemplifies how well animals can evolve adaptations to withstand the rigors of winter.

Although it is widespread in the Canadian subarctic evergreen forest, the lynx's range in northeastern United States is limited to a few areas. In Maine, this rare cat is thought to live only in the headwaters of the Allagash, St. John, and Penobscot rivers.

If there were a ghost in this forest, the lynx would be a good candidate. Furtive and elusive, it is rarely seen in the wild. One was reported near Lock Dam on Chamberlain Lake in the late sixties or early seventies.[4] Signs of its presence, such as scratching posts, scat, and tracks, are often inconspicuous. Even in winter, when tracking is at its best, thick hairs on the cat's feet produce indistinct toe prints.

The lynx is not a stranger to cold. In fact, some believe that it entered the Americas six hundred thousand years ago during the Ice Age. Its long, soft, insulating fur prepares it well for surviving the Allagash's coldest and snowiest month—January. This is when plants and animals are put to the test. The

In Maine the lynx is now thought to reside principally in the remote headwaters of the Allagash, St. John, and Penobscot rivers. The gray jay sometimes gives agitated warning calls upon spotting a lynx.

average on these January days hovers around twelve degrees Fahrenheit, and it may be much colder. During such times, the lynx is able to go a week without food by remaining motionless in a protected spot.

As a carnivore, the lynx is ideally suited for stalking and capturing its favorite prey, the snowshoe hare (*Lepus americanus*). Stiff hairs on the bottom of its oversized, four-inch-wide feet provide easier walking and running on deep, soft snow. Patience and climbing ability give it the advantage of ambush. Long tufts on its ears convey the slightest sound, and a keen sense of smell enables it to pick up the faintest scent. Its eyes are located in front of its skull for binocular vision and are adapted to seeing in the dark. Without these specialties, the lynx would have little success hunting in the jumble of thickets, wind-thrown trees, moss-covered boulders, gullies, and streams that make up the forest floor in these north woods.

The lynx generally hunts a range of six to eight square miles, and like most mammals does its hunting mainly at night when the hares are active. Once the lynx spots its prey, its lithe muscular body and long legs allow it to move fast and leap as much as twelve to fifteen feet. A hare has little chance if it comes within reach of the cat's one-and-a-quarter-inch-long, recurved, needle-sharp claws.

So inextricably is the lynx's survival tied to the snowshoe hare's population cycle (its diet is 80 to 90 percent hare, or about one per day) that its population rises and falls with the hare's. When hares are scarce, the lynx must make do with animals such as the deer mouse (*Peromyscus maniculatus*), red squirrel (*Tamiasciurus hudsonicus*), chipmunk (*Tamias striatus*), ruffed grouse (*Bonasa umbellus*), and spruce grouse.

Such is the nature of the region where the Allagash has its origin. A transit of the Allagash Waterway begins here, at the river's wild and remote headwaters. It is the beginning of a passage through a remnant of the north woods, where one can still capture some of the flavor of the forest when it existed during an earlier, wilder time.

The Upper Stream

Winter maintains tight control over the rivulets and brooks in the hilly country northwest of Allagash Mountain. Temperature is the dam keeper, storing the winter's accumulating snow and determining when the gates will open. As spring approaches and the days begin to warm, the hold is loosened. The sounds of the first trickles on the southfacing slopes are muffled by the snow, but inevitably the changes become more perceptible. By May icy water is flowing down hills and small, twisting valleys. The weather, the slope of the land, and the forest exercise major control over the increasing torrent.

SPRING HAVOC

Eleven miles upstream from Allagash Lake and fourteen feet higher, the runoff fills Allagash Pond and pushes against the thick ice floating on its surface. The stream overflows its banks. Cakes of floating ice and forest debris from the ravages of winter sweep downstream, creating havoc along its banks—peeling the bark from overhanging trees and breaking limbs and trunks. Logs and sticks swirl into eddies, catch on sharp turns, and lodge in backwaters. Jams build up, then break apart, dispatching erratic pulses of uncontrolled energy. The streambed shifts and re-forms as boulders dislodge and sands and gravels wash into pools and create beaches and bars. Occasionally, banks are carved away and trees fall into the rushing stream.

Youthful and fast, the stream flows along the path of least resistance. An ancient fault runs parallel to the stream near its south side, appearing to influence the last three miles of the stream's route to Allagash Lake. This break and subsequent movement in the bedrock separates the volcanic formations of the Allagash Mountain area just south of the stream from the dark gray slate that underlies its bed and the land to its north.

On a micro scale, the spring runoff continues the massive earthwork abandoned by the glacier, which exerted its influence longer here than elsewhere in Maine. Evidence suggests that these headwaters and the lakes and lower stretches of the river below are among those areas where the glacier, already diminished, made its final stand in the state some eleven thousand years ago. A thousand years later, Maine was free of ice, climaxing the three thousand years or so that it took to reduce the mammoth sheet to meltwater. The process had a dramatic effect here in the lowlands, much different from the erosive shaping and polishing of the bedrock seen on the top of Allagash Mountain. Millions of tons of bedrock were imported by meltwater currents and stocked in calm waters. Now the stream, in its comparatively slow, puttering way, works on the material, adding a little here, taking away there, but all the time making its own mark on the landscape.

Spring thaws loosen winter's hold on the brooks and streams that feed the Allagash headwaters.

Today the work-in-progress reveals a stream that, upon first leaving Allagash Pond, meanders through gently sloping wetlands located on deposits of sand and gravel left at the front of the glacier's receding ice margin. As the slope increases, the stream turns sharply to the left and follows the configuration of the faulted bedrock through glacial materials. Three miles below Allagash Pond the stream's bed slopes more gently, becoming almost flat, and the stream slows and meanders in a manner typical of a river nearing its mouth. Here alluvial terraces, fan-shaped deposits, and floodplains of sand, gravel, and silt made within the past eight thousand years reflect a recent geologic time called the Holocene.

Allagash Stream winds its way through a dense forest in the remote headwaters of the river.

BURST OF LIFE

The complex interactions between land and water occurring along this tiny, remote stream, set and shaped by crustal movement and glacial activity, provide the stage on which a myriad of living things play out their roles. Here and along the entire hundred-mile stretch of water below, each species finds its special requirements for space, food, water, and protection. The waterway offers perhaps the greatest diversity of habitats of any river system in the Northeast, each locality exhibiting its own uniqueness and sometimes harboring species rarely found elsewhere.

Changes come posthaste in the north woods when spring arrives. The runoff washes nutrients from the forest floor into the stream; and as the days lengthen and warm, the cold, oxygen-loaded waters are prepared for the flurry of plant and animal activity to come.

Many animals live where the current is fast and turbulent—in the rocky, gravel-bottomed rapids and riffles and along the outsides of curves. Where they take up residence is likely to be influenced more by their adaptations to current than by any other single factor. Body shapes tend to be low profiled and streamlined, with special devices for attachment to rocks. Here sponges (phylum Porifera) encrust the rocks, and small flatworms (phylum Platyhelminthes) feed beneath them where they are protected from the current. Stone fly nymphs (order Plecoptera) crawl about the stones, their flattened bodies oriented headfirst against the force of moving water. Mayfly nymphs (order Ephemeroptera) also forage along the stream's bottom. The larvae of net-veined midges (family Blephariceridae) and the flattened round larvae of water-penny beetles (family Psephenidae) are also well adapted to this quick-water environment. Many of the animals are similar in appearance, representing an evolutionary convergence of form. Even the larvae of caddis flies (order Trichoptera), which inhabit the riffle areas, build solid, protective cases of sand that are stream-lined to withstand the current.

These north woods streams are also infamous for their production of black flies (family Simuliidae), the scourge of warm-blooded animals, including humans. C.H. Hitchcock, reporting in 1862 on the first geological exploration of the Allagash Lake area by Oliver White, wrote that White's "zeal was the more to be commended since the abundance of venomous insects rendered exposure to their attacks almost insufferable."[5] Sixty years later George Kephart, a forester who came into this region in 1919, gave a more graphic description:

> On one of these [spring] days, after a night of rain, I was stone-hopping my way across Allagash Stream, at this point no more than a brook. In midstream I paused, partly to look ahead for the next stepping stone, but mostly to enjoy the picture of clean, fresh water tumbling down under an archway of new green. With mild annoyance I brushed aside a tiny fly that hovered around my face. Then, suddenly, a cloud of vicious little black flies was all around me. They probed into eyes, nose, and ears, and raised painful welts on all exposed surfaces as they slaked their thirst with my blood. Brushing them away became an act of flailing and futile desperation, and there was the same impulse to run that comes over one who blunders into a yellow jacket nest.[6]

Interspersed between the riffles are the quieter waters of pools. In these places the stream slows and fine sands, silts, and clays settle out, building a softer streambed. Temperature is higher, oxygen is lower, and the bottoms are less stable than the rocky rapids. In these respects, pools are similar to lake environments. Here, away from the stress of fast currents and

faced with a different set of habitat conditions, animals adopt different shapes and strategies for survival. Sponges exhibit branched and tube shapes. Freshwater mussels (class Pelecypoda) burrow in the sediments, filtering tiny floating plants and animals. Nymphs of mayflies, dragonflies (suborder Anisoptera), and damselflies (suborder Zygoptera), which are especially adapted to pool conditions, burrow in the sediments

The hardy wood frog is adapted to the cold climate of the north woods. Except during breeding season, when it seeks out wet areas, it lives in cool, moist woods.

A male brook trout displays the bright coloration of the breeding season. Lake populations of brook trout seek out cold tributaries in the waterway for spawning.

and lurk in the vegetation. Water striders (family Gerridae), water boatmen (family Corixidae), back swimmers (family Notonectidae), and whirligig beetles (family Gyrinidae) gather here. And where pools are stagnant, mosquito larvae (family Culicidae) develop and hatch.

Spring is also a time when pools and backwaters become the musical breeding grounds of amphibians. The vocalizations of spring peepers (*Pseudacris crucifer*) are heard first, followed by the wood frogs (*Rana sylvatica*). And then, in approximate order, American toads, pickerel frogs (*Rana palustris*), northern leopard frogs (*Rana pipiens*), green frogs (*Rana clamitans*), bullfrogs (*Rana catesbeiana*), and, finally, mink frogs (*Rana septentrionalis*).

This is also an important time in the reproductive cycles of fish. Suckers, white (*Catostomus commersoni*) and longnose (*Catostomus catostomus*), come up the stream from the lake below to spawn, splashing and rolling in the shallow, gravel-bottomed riffles. In early spring, before the full force of the runoff is under way, tiny brook trout (*Salvelinus fontinalis*), called fry, squirm up through the loose gravel covering the nests where their mothers buried eggs the previous fall.

Changes also come to the trees and shrubs lining the banks of the stream. Spruces and firs begin adding new growth of twigs that bristle with bright green needles. Overhanging speckled alders (*Alnus rugosa*) leaf out and provide shade, which will become important to the brook trout in summer when the sun tends to warm the cool waters and limit available oxygen the trout need.

Along the stream beaver (*Castor canadensis*) begin their work of repairing dams and building new ones, favoring such natural barriers as downed trees and rocky ledges as building sites. Banks reveal trails and slides leading to the gnawed-off stubs of alders. Floating alder branches and stems with orange, freshly chewed ends give clues to the nocturnal activities of this large rodent.

A SUMMER STREAM

As summer arrives and progresses, the high waters of spring subside and reveal slate-gray rocks in the upper reaches of the stream; humps breaking the surface glare in riffles of the swiftly moving water. Little if anything is long unused in nature.

The receding waters have scarcely uncovered the streambed's boulders before avian designs, rendered in the pigment *excrementum* white, appear—the unintentional but provocative artistic embellishments of roosting birds.

At the water's edge, spotted sandpipers (*Actitis macularia*) bob among the pebbles and rocks, hunting for insects, trout fry, and small crustaceans. These "teeter-tails" move quickly, picking their way along the shore, then, with wings stiff and down curled, flying short distances to explore new stretches of shore.

The summer stream slows and its waters lower. Around many of the bends' inside curves, high, mounded gravel bars, indented by the sharp hooves of white-tailed deer (*Odocoileus virginianus*) and moose, obscure views down the stream. On gently sloping, marshy, and often unstable banks of sand and other fine materials blue flag (*Iris versicolor*) makes a regal impression among the tall grasses. With moisture and light favoring lush plant growth, this member of the iris family, like the cattails (*Typha latifolia*), has adopted a growth strategy of putting the greater amount of energy and nutrients into reproduction. It produces an abundance of flowers on tall, leafy stems to better ensure the survival of some of its many seeds in a fickle environment.

Above the stretch of deep deadwater leading into Allagash lake, the stream enters a new phase of life—one of exaggerated meandering. The twisting channel propels the flow of water into the outside curves of the stream's banks, undercutting the sandy, silty soil. Gravelly pools become larger, deeper, and more frequent. Graying logs, uprooted by turbulent floodwaters and battered by floating debris, line the shore, providing sunning spots for "ole redlegs," the wood turtle (*Clemmys insculpta*).

Overhead, the kinked wings of ospreys (*Pandion haliaetus*) maneuver abrupt turns, their presence suggesting that a lake is close by. Here, too, American bitterns (*Botaurus lentiginosus*) follow the meandering stream. At one angle, silhouetted against the sky, they might be mistaken for one of the herring gulls (*Larus argentatus*) that are often heard calling in the distance.

Near the lake a high ridge appears on the left. Large openings between the trees show a forest disturbed by the

Along the upper section of Allagash Stream, cuttings and dams made by beavers are a common sight.

force of high, gusty winds sweeping through the valley. Blocked by the rise of land, the stream turns abruptly right and exposes a small, low ledge, which gives a glimpse of the upthrust bedrock that forms the ridge. In the concealing forest it's the streams that cut through the cover of soil to reveal the secret nature of the rock foundation below. Here the ledge outcrop is clutched by the roots of a towering white pine. The lichen-covered, gray rock is striped with parallel bands, an indelibly scoured record of the stream's fluctuating levels.

The stretch of deadwater follows along the ridge. To the right, the land is flat and mucky—a floodplain thick with clumps of speckled alders. They grow in the muck of the nutrient-rich, oxygenated water. Bacteria in the shrub's roots fix nitrogen, adding to the fertility of the soil.

Among the marsh grasses along the shore of the sluggish, widening stream, families of American black ducks (*Anas rubripes*) feed. Adults guard fuzzy-headed ducklings while they "tip up" for five to seven seconds at a time to probe the bottom for submerged pondweeds and aquatic insects. Common loons (*Gavia immer*) also swim up from the lake to fish in the deepest water where the stream's channel cuts into the bed of the deadwater.

Where the stream enters Allagash Lake, it laps against a long, jutting, slate outcrop—the ridge once again brought to light and scoured by spring freshets. Here the hidden structure of the ridge becomes clearer. The former sedimentary layers of silt and clay, now metamorphosed by heat and pressure, incline to a nearly vertical eighty degrees, their exposed edges running in a line northeast by southwest. A heavy coat of mosses and lichens on the outcrop's glacially worn, vertical face shows evidence of scouring by high water. Spruces and balsam fir cling to the ledge's top, and in the summer bright red blossoms of sheep laurel (*Kalmia angustifolia*) blaze the entrance of the stream into the lake.

A short distance back from the stream's mouth, a shallow, weedy backwater sits protected between the upstream end of the ledge and a strip of alders on the stream's north bank. Moose, deer, loons, and ducks feed in the shallow, quiet waters of this secluded spot. Along the south bank of the stream, another strip of alders grows on fine-grained floodwater sediments, which settle out as the stream enters the lake, slows, and loses its carrying capacity. The bar extends into the lake and fans out in delta fashion beneath the water's surface, only a few emerging blades of marsh grass marking its shallow depth. The stream now becomes a part of Allagash Lake.

The Lake

Remote and completely natural, Allagash Lake is a lake of unusual beauty. Its basin and irregular shoreline display strikingly beautiful effects of volcanic and glacial activity. But its most powerful aspect is the impression it gives as an undisturbed lake of true wilderness.

Compared with other lakes in the region, Allagash Lake is modest in size. Covering a total of 4,360 acres, its waters span three and one-half miles west to east and four miles north to south. And in keeping with many lakes of the north woods, it is deep—eighty-nine feet at its deepest point and averaging thirty-five feet. Water below the thirty-foot level, even in summer, is cold and well oxygenated and contains an unusually high diversity of cold-water fish—brook trout; lake trout, or togue (*Salvelinus namaycush*); cusk, or burbot (*Lota lota*); lake whitefish (*Coregonus clupeaformis*); round whitefish (*Prosopium cylindraceum*); and longnose sucker. The white sucker is also present, and, preferring warmer waters, inhabits the shallows of inlets.

DEEP WATERS

Like the surrounding forest, the lake's waters and its life are strongly influenced by the climate and seasonal changes. Each spring breakup leads to conditions favorable for the cold-water fish. George Kephart gives a firsthand account of this phenomenon as he witnessed it here in 1919:

> The real spring Breakup was often heralded by an all-day or all-night rain. Then the waterlogged snow would begin to disintegrate and each tiny brook would cascade its addition into the larger streams which, in turn, became clamorous with floodwaters. There was the swish of low-lying branches, buried all winter under the snow, as they were released from their burdens and sprang back to normal position. Water came

> up over the lake ice and made it no longer safe to walk on. Finally the ice broke up, and there was again the sound of waves washing against the shore. Throughout the forest the stillness of winter gave way to the sounds of Nature's awakening.[7]

When the ice leaves the lake in early to mid-May, the surface water gradually warms from its temperature of thirty-two degrees Fahrenheit. Strangely, the water becomes heavier as it warms above freezing. Simply explained, it's a matter of

A bald eagle catches a brook trout in Allagash Lake. Some of Maine's northernmost-nesting bald eagles breed in the Allagash Wilderness Waterway.

the changing density of water molecules. When frozen, the molecules are farther apart and held rigidly in a latticework arrangement. As the water warms above freezing, the structure breaks down, and the molecules draw closer together, packing into a smaller space. At 39.2 degrees Fahrenheit the surface water reaches its maximum density and, weighing more than the colder water beneath it, sinks. The colder, lighter water below rises, and when it, too, warms to 39.2 degrees, it sinks. Thus, all of the water in the lake eventually becomes nearly the same temperature of 39.2 degrees and is easily mixed when subjected to wind. The mixing is called the "spring overturn" and is especially critical to the cold-water fish because it serves to carry oxygen throughout the lake's waters.

During the summer, thermal stratification keeps the lower waters cold and well oxygenated. The lake's surface waters warm and form a layer lighter in weight that floats on the colder waters below. Beneath this upper layer is a zone where the water rapidly cools until a depth is reached at which the temperature remains fairly uniformly cold—as low as thirty-nine degrees Fahrenheit or a few degrees above. It is here that the cold-water fish live.

In the fall the process is reversed, and a fall overturn takes place, replenishing the waters with oxygen that must sustain the fish through the winter until the spring overturn. In Allagash Lake fall is the time when brook trout and whitefish move to the stream to spawn while lake trout congregate around shallow gravel-bottomed or ledgy shoals. The burbot, however, wait until midwinter to spawn beneath the ice.

ENCHANTING SHORES

The varied shoreline of Allagash Lake contributes much to its interest and charm. During spring and summer the shallow waters and marshy edges of its inlet cove attract deer and moose. Dawn and dusk activate their visits, a time when the cove's calm surface frets from their wading, the ripples often mingling with those from trout rising after mayflies. The insects hatch at their peril, but in nature's evenhandedness the pursuing trout are also in danger, for bald eagles (*Haliæetus leucocephalus*) and ospreys hunt here too.

From the eagle's vantage, a defining feature of the cove occurs a short distance down the north shore where the north-bounding ridge of slate makes a short incursion into the lake. Back from the water's edge among the spruce and fir and near a moss-covered outcrop, summer brings forth the colorful blossoms of twinflower (*Linnaea borealis*). Huddled close to the ground, this delicate evergreen's trailing stems give rise to short upright branches that terminate in a matched pair of

Near Allagash Lake, the delicate blossoms of twinflower catch a ray of sunlight. This low, creeping evergreen plant of cool woods and bogs sends up tiny branched stalks topped by pairs of small flowers.

pinkish white, bell-shaped flowers. Unlike the seed-bearing strategy of blue flag, which produces large, abundant flowers to propagate new populations as insurance against unstable environments, twinflower puts its energy into the growth of leaves, stems, and roots. In the forest, where its environment is less changeable, this strategy is aimed at enabling each individual plant to better survive the rigors of winter.

Beyond the inlet cove along the north shore, Mile Brook enters at a point where for thousands of years it has carried fine sands from the low, surrounding hills to the edge of the lake. Here, shore currents have slowly and gently distributed them over the bottom and along the shoreline, building a long beach and sandy shallows extending for hundreds of feet out into the lake. Gradually a few marsh grasses and aquatic plants have gained a foothold, inviting deer and moose. On the sandy bottom their tracks intermingle with those of the great blue heron (*Ardea herodias*). This is the littoral zone, where sunlight penetrates to the bottom and encourages the growth of aquatic plants. But in this particular place the unstable, shifting sands negate the sunlight's effect, accounting for the sparseness of aquatic plant growth.

Across the lake the strikingly dissimilar west shore gives open testimony to nature's evolving diversity. The rough, rocky shore is high and steep

with low ledges extending outward before plunging into the lake. Fine-grained, gray basalt of the Allagash Lake Formation constitutes much of the bedrock. In places the fractured rock mass appears pillow shaped and broken along joint planes in a blocklike texture. Iron staining from the mineral hematite gives the dark rock an earthy reddish color. Close up, as on the mountains, the rock displays green fragments of the mineral epidote and tiny veins of igneous intrusions. The patterning is further enhanced by thin layers of grayish red sandstone, pebble conglomerate, and limestone created from carbonate mud and the broken skeletons of ancient shell life. Occasional crystals of quartz project from the rock, impervious to the assault of water and weather. In summer, the ledges

With its sharply pointed bill and long neck and legs, the great blue heron is uniquely equipped for catching fish, frogs, and other small aquatic creatures. It is often seen in the waterway, standing motionless in shallow waters and wetlands.

are painted with white waterlines, showing the erosive effect of wave action and providing a permanent record of the lake's fluctuating levels.

In other places along this unusual shore, small nubbly islands rise out of the water, some of which guard hidden inlets and coves with reedy pocket beaches. Here the waves jostle polished pebbles of calcite, basalt, quartz, and, occasionally, gray-white banded gneiss brought by the glacier from the Canadian Shield to the north. Yet, in spite of the tranquillity of this shore—the dried exoskeletons of dragonfly nymphs resting quietly on its rocks, the smoothing valances of cedars and firs over its lichen-covered ledges, and its barren, glacially polished outcrops—the evidence of a violent history is readily apparent.

A 400-million-year-old outcrop of volcanic pillow lava breaks the surface of Allagash Lake along the western shore.

The theory of how this fascinating shoreline formed contains many parallels with the geologic history of the entire north woods region.[8] It's a story that requires imagining almost inconceivably large scales of time and physical dimension. The idea of continents drifting on the surface of the planet is central to understanding what happened here.

Beginning some 500 million years ago, at least two large bodies of the earth's crust collided with this continent. Following this period events occurred that left in their wake the bedrock formation now existing as Allagash Mountain, Poland Mountain, and others forming the shore and region west of the lake. Some 410 to 415 million years ago, in a time period called the late Silurian, a sinking of the earth's crust took place in this region, and a large ocean basin was formed. Present-day Allagash Lake is located where the edge of this ancient sea once lay. Volcanic eruptions occurred along this coastline, and pulses of lava measuring several thousand feet across, perhaps up to a mile, flowed into the ocean. Underwater cooling created pillowlike forms of the basalt. Some lava flowed onto the land above sea level and cooled into rough, jagged rock forms called clinkers. During intervals between lava flows, layers of sediments were deposited onto the solidified lava layers, and can be seen today as thin, interbedded layers of metamorphosed sedimentary rock in the basalt.

The bedrock geology of the area still was not complete. During the millions of years that followed the volcanic development of the Allagash Formation, mountains bordering the regional inland sea slowly eroded. Fine sediments of sand, silt, and clay accumulated in the deep water of the sea's basin to depths of two to three miles. The enormous pressure generated by the weight of the materials solidified them into mudstone, siltstone, and other sedimentary rocks. However, the pressure was nothing compared with what the rocks experienced some 390 million years ago when the ancient European continent of Baltica, nearing the end of its slow, fateful course toward the Old North American continent, added a final land-mass, called Avalonia, to Maine. This collision, known as the Acadian Orogeny, crunched the continent, crumpling and metamorphosing the bedrock. The sea disappeared, and its deep-water basin of sedimentary rock was changed to a meta-morphic rock group called Seboomook Slate. This gray, lay-ered rock now forms much of the bedrock east and north of Allagash Lake.

THE ICE CAVE

One of the interesting results of the geologic activity on the shore of this lake is found near the top of a high, rocky knoll rising 180 feet above the mouth of the inlet cove. On the north side of the knoll, facing the lake, a gaping dark crevice slashes down into the hillside. On warm days a cold mist drifts up from the damp depths below. The cool, moist air attracts wood frogs, among other creatures. Their dark eye masks somehow seem fitting to the mysteriousness of this place. In the fall bats seek out the cave for winter hibernation.

Inside the cave's entrance, the rocky floor of the down-ward-sloping passage is steep and muddy. Sharp, jutting rocks line the tunnel. The temperature drops rapidly on descent, and moisture condenses on the rock surfaces. Thirty feet down, the cave opens into a large room about twenty feet long by ten feet wide and eight to ten feet high. It is close, cool, and dark. A dim shaft of light marks the location of the entrance above. In the dead quiet, sounds are hollow and reverberate off the rock walls. Two crevicelike tunnels, large enough to explore, branch off on opposite sides of the room. They pen-etrate the hillside to depths where ice remains year-round. The jumble of rocks and broken, displaced sections of ledge that surround the room and create the tunnels give further evi-dence of the powerful geologic forces once at work here.

THE HIDDEN BOG

Nestled in wet depressions throughout the headwaters region are examples of another interesting natural feature: the boreal peat bog. Near Allagash Lake a classic example lies hidden in a small basin of volcanic rock at the base of a sixty-foot ledge.

The wetland resembles a typical kettlehole bog with a fifty-foot-wide floating mat of heaths and sphagnum moss sur-rounding a small body of open water. This wetland, however, appears to have originated in a natural depression of bedrock. The true kettlehole bog is formed quite differently: a chunk of ice breaks off from a stagnating or retreating glacier and is buried in meltwater deposits of sands or gravels; when the ice melts it leaves a water-filled depression that, over time, may develop into a peat bog.

Regardless of its origin, this beautiful, secluded bog developed because of a situation common in northern ponds—poor drainage in combination with a deficiency of nutrients and oxygen. In this small mountain basin of water, northern plants found their niche, adapted as they are to poor nutri-ent conditions and a short growing season of less than one hundred days, a characteristic also of exposed lowlands in these northern areas. Along the quiet shoreline of the tiny, pro-tected pond, the destabilizing effects of heavy wave action were absent, and the plants began to grow.

The ubiquitous leatherleaf (*Chamaedaphne calyculata*) was undoubtedly one of the first to invade the edge of the pond from which the bog developed; it laid the foundation for the surrounding mat. This plant, like other members of the heath family, is able to thrive in wet, low-nutrient situations. And like many of the heaths, it bears leaves year-round, thus coping with the short growing season and retaining the energy that would otherwise be needed to grow new leaves each year. The leaves resist water loss during dry periods by being thick and hairy, and their slender, oblong shape exposes a small sur-

The orchid calopogon, or grass-pink, grows in acid bogs, as does the black spruce, seen here behind the orchid. Calopogon's blossom appears to be upside down; unlike most orchids, which have a lower petal in the form of a crested lip, calopogon's lip is at the top.

face area in relation to their volume. Leatherleaf grows vigorously and can form a dense tangle of roots and stems outward from the pond's edge. Where cool conditions and low oxygen levels prevail, decay processes slow, and the formation of peat begins.

Once the foundation of dead and live vegetation had been provided, sphagnum moss (*Sphagnum* spp.) accelerated the formation of the bog. Sphagnum is especially adapted to the wet environments of the north woods. It can hold ten to twenty times its weight in water. Its cells absorb mineral bases

while setting hydrogen ions free, thus contributing to the acidity of the water. The measure of acidity is termed *pH* for the number of possible hydrogen ions present. In northern bogs the pH is typically 3.3 to 4.5, or very acid (a pH of 7 is neutral). Their high acidity in combination with the absorption of minerals by the sphagnum limits the availability of nutrients.

As the mat developed, other plants also gained a foothold. These include other heaths—blueberry (*Vaccinium* spp.), small cranberry (*Vaccinium oxycoccus*), and Labrador tea (*Ledum groenlandicum*). Trees and shrubs began to take root in the accumulating soil on the open mat around the edge of the bog. One of the first was black spruce. Intolerant to shade and adapted to low-nutrient, wet conditions, it advanced out onto the expanding mat, with the potential of turning the bog into a forest. The tree's wide-spreading, shallow root system penetrates the upper mat where oxygen exists, and it has the ability to produce new trees from branches that grow roots when they are buried in the accumulating sphagnum. The black spruce was also joined by shrubs such as speckled alder. And out on the mat, between the trees and shrubs and the slowly shrinking pond in the center, a number of very unusual plants found a home. These are the orchids and carnivorous plants.

By mid-July orchids dot the tiny bog with bright colors. The beautiful rose-purple-colored calopogon, or grass-pink (*Calopogon pulchellus*), is one of these. Unlike most orchids, which have a lower petal in the form of a crested, hairy lip, this orchid's lip is upright on the top. Another pink orchid growing on the bog is rose pogonia, or snake-mouth (*Pogonia ophioglossoides*). Its perfumed flower shows off a fringed lower lip crested with yellow hairs. Also found here is the exquisite white fringed orchis (*Habenaria blephariglottis*). Taller than the others, its pure white flowers each have a deeply fringed lower petal and a long spur curving downward.

The sexual adaptations of the orchids are most amaz-

ing. The ends to which they have gone in their long love affair with pollinating animals, especially the insects, are truly incredible. By customizing its color, shape, and scent to the desires and anatomy of a specific insect who alone is able to facilitate the fertilization of its eggs, an orchid is able to ensure that its pollen is transferred to another of its kind and thus achieve its cross-fertilization. For example, rose pogonia's violetlike fragrance and its fringed lower lip are designed to attract a bee. Upon alighting and entering the flower, the bee is pressed tightly against the upper surface of the opening. In backing out, the bee's head catches pollen that it carries to the next flower.

The pollination strategy of grass-pink, with its upright, crested upper lip, is less obvious. Compared with other orchids, which have large, attractive lower petals, it appears ill-equipped—until a carpenter bee (subfamily Xylocopinae) happens along and succumbs to the temptations offered by this seducer. The bee, seeing the yellow hairlike "stamens" on the upright lip (which possibly suggest the presence of nectar, though none exists) swoops down and lands. Immediately the hinged lip folds down, and the bee falls over into a glob of pollen in a cradle formed by the sexual organs of the orchid. As the bee struggles to extricate itself, the pollen sticks to its back. Once free, the bee flies off to another plant and the stratagem repeats itself, leaving pollen on the next orchid's stigma.

Unlike grass-pink and rose pogonia, the white fringed orchis does have nectar. It is located in a long spur suspended below the flower. Only the long tongue of a hummingbird or a moth can reach the sweet liquid. And the design of the flower is such that the nectar can be obtained only when the pollinator is in a position that guarantees that its head picks up pollen and can deliver it properly to the next flower.

When an orchid's dust-size seeds develop following pol-

The white fringed orchis, tall and delicately formed, makes a regal appearance on the wetlands.

The spatulate-leaved sundew grows in acid bogs and may be found at the water's edge of a bog mat. Its white blossoms and reddish foliage contrast with the yellow flowers of the horned bladderwort.

lination, thousands from each flower are strewn over the bog by the wind. Their small size means that the seeds do not contain a large supply of stored food for the tiny plants that will eventually sprout from them, and one might wonder how they could survive and grow. They wouldn't if it were not for an invading fungus from which the orchid seedlings are able to obtain additional food.

Equally astonishing, in comparison with the orchids, are the peculiar adaptations of another completely different group—the carnivorous plants. Three of these insect eaters live

on the mat and at the water's edge of this hidden bog—pitcher plant (*Sarracenia purpurea*), spatulate-leaved sundew (*Drosera intermedia*), and horned bladderwort (*Utricularia cornuta*). Why do these unusual members of the plant kingdom trap and digest insects? Simply put, the plants need vitamin supplements, especially when reproducing and essential nutrients, particularly nitrogen, are in short supply.

Studies have shown that up to 40 percent of the nitrogen in a pitcher plant's roots comes from insects. How the plant acquires this essential nutrient—with an intricate assemblage of cell-built structures seemingly based on an uncanny comprehension of insect behavior—is one of nature's great accomplishments. The basic structure of the plant consists of leaves funneling up from the roots to form vases. The bright red, veined patterns and the nectar glands in this pitcher-shaped structure are the first to capture the attention of a hungry insect. The flared top is an open invitation to enter, and downward-aimed hairs assist the unsuspecting victim in its descent to a point where slippery footing is encountered. The inevitable mad scramble to keep from sliding into the pool of collected rainwater below dislodges cells that stick to the insect, further hindering its escape, and it slides into the liquid to meet its death by drowning. Enzymes and bacteria initiate digestion, and eventually the nutrients obtained through the process are absorbed into the plant.

As might be expected, the pitcher plant itself provides a habitat for animals. A small mosquito, the larva of a fly, and a small wasp are all known to inhabit the pitcher and successfully avoid entrapment. Some species of spiders weave webs across the flared top of the pitcher to intercept insects. Small tree frogs also have been seen sitting on the rims of pitcher plants, waiting to capture insects attracted to them.

Near the water, along the edge of the mat, spatulate-leaved sundew plants and horned bladderworts thrive. In July the small white flowers and red, glistening, droplet-bearing leaves of the sundews and the intensely yellow blossoms of the bladderworts brighten the shoreline. The sparkling, colorful sundews bestow a jeweled appearance to the mat's ragged edge. The jewels, however, are deadly drops of sticky liquid on the ends of glandular, tentaclelike hairs that can trap an unsuspecting insect, ensnare it, and, if it struggles, completely wrap around it in twenty minutes. After administering an anesthetic and digesting its prey with secreted enzymes, the plant opens and resets its trap.

The horned bladderwort possesses a very refined mechanism for trapping insects. Lacking roots, the plant's support comes entirely from the stem and the finely divided leaves, which have tiny sacs on them called bladders. The bladders are slightly collapsed and maintain a partial vacuum inside. Door-like flaps over their openings seal out the surrounding water. If a small organism, such as a water flea (order Cladocera) or a mosquito larva, gets too close to a bladder and touches a trigger, the flap opens and the prey is washed inside with the entering surge of water. Fifteen minutes to two hours later, after enzymes and bacteria have completed the digestion process, the water is pumped back out and the trap is readied again.

A wetland such as this hidden bog is visited by many other animals in addition to spiders and insects. Above its surface flycatchers and tree swallows dart and swoop. And around its perimeter, deer and moose leave rutted trails in the soft, wet soil.

THE DISAPPEARING COVE

Down the western shore of the lake, in the shadow of Allagash Mountain, the conversion of a cove into another interesting but different wetland is well under way. From the edge of the

A spring peeper tree frog sits on the rim of a pitcher plant, perhaps to intercept an insect attracted by the carnivorous plant's red lip and nectar glands.

lake a shallow stream, thickly bordered by low woody shrubs, winds its way into the wetland. At the stream's edge, near the top of the low leafy cover, the bright pink blossoms of northeastern, or shiny, rose (*Rosa nitida*) dance in the breeze. The slow-moving stream opens into a small, shallow pond, a remnant of the once larger cove. Beneath its few inches of water lies dark brown muck many feet deep as measured by moose who sink almost from sight as they feed in the pond and struggle to move in its mire. The pond's years are numbered by the accumulating sediments and the closing circle of shrubs at its edge.

On the surrounding bog mat an open forest of scattered northern white cedar has replaced the black spruce common to the pioneering forests of many peatlands in the north woods. The white cedar is more tolerant of shade and grows better on sites that are less acid and more nutrient rich. Like the black spruce, it can reproduce by layering—rooting and growing new shoots in the thickening blanket of sphagnum moss. In this wetland, hummocks interspersed among pools of water provide homes for pitcher plants, rose pogonias, and cottongrass (*Eriophorum virginicum*). On the cedar trees, hanging beard lichen (*Usnea* sp.) waves in the breezes. A ridge rises above the wetland at its northern edge; here a large dead white pine provides a favorite perch for bald eagles.

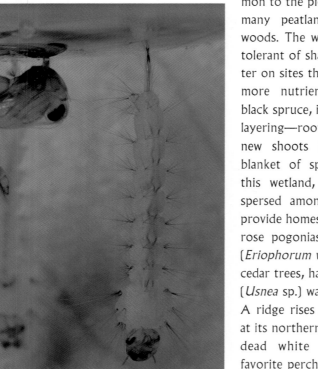

The tiny pitcher plant mosquito lays its eggs in the nutrient-rich pool of rainwater collected inside a pitcher plant. The larva on the right has extended its breathing tube to the surface. In the foreground is a pupa, the stage between larva and adult.

Tern and Gull Islands

Much of the enchantment of northern lakes derives from their diverse environments and the life they support. Where the wetlands are closed, secluded, and full of hidden surprises, the opposite is true of the islands. Allagash Lake has three unnamed islands that are especially distinctive because of their bird populations.

"Tern Island" is a low, glacier-worked hump of ledge and jumbled boulders rising out of the lake just east of the inlet cove. Its sparse vegetation includes a few small shrubs. To the northwest, only a short distance away, a small, low, glacially smoothed companion island breaks the surface waters during the summer months when the lake is low.

There are parallels to human history on "Tern Island." At one time common terns (*Sterna hirundo*) seemed to have exclusive colonization rights to the entire island. Eventually, however, a nearby population of herring gulls, in search of an isolated, predator-free island to accommodate their expanding numbers, decided to invade. The terns, small and slight of build, were no match in the face-off with the larger, aggressive gulls. The result: at times the island appears to have an imaginary truce zone separating its northern and southern halves. There can be no mistaking who controls which side— the gulls "flag" the rocks on their side of the island with great washes of white excrement. The eventual takeover by the gulls may be inevitable; the conflict is a classic one that terns everywhere have been losing.

The swallowlike terns cruise over the shallower areas of the lake, perhaps twenty to fifty feet above the surface, their long red-orange bills pointing downward and black-capped heads turning from side to side as they search for small fish. When a fish is spotted, a tern will hover by rapidly beating its long, graceful wings and extending its forked tail. Then it plunges in an arrowlike dive headfirst into the water, snatching the fish in its bill. Quickly emerging, it swallows the fish or carries it back to the island to feed its young.

There is much activity around the island during June through August when the young are being raised. White flashes of wings and harsh calls of adults surround the island while the young terns huddle in niches in the rocks waiting to be fed. In the evening the raucous noise increases, as it does when intruders are spotted. If danger appears imminent, the tern chicks will take to the water. Most of the visitors to the island, however, are harmless birds, and as fall approaches these increase as migrations from farther north begin. Semipalmated sandpipers (*Calidris pusilla*), for example, are known to stop and rest on the island.

A little more than two miles away, near the southeast shore of the lake, is one of two gull islands, where the main colony of herring gulls resides. Thick, chunky, upturned layers of weathered and broken slate align the low, elongated island north and south. Near the shore, tufts of grass and woody shrubs exhibit a stubborn will to survive between ice-wedged, pushed-apart beds of the dark rock. Away from the wave-washed, scoured edge, shrubs grow more profusely and spruce take over, dominating the center of the island. Many of the trees are as much as thirty feet high. Ornamenting their tops are noisy, brilliantly white-headed gulls. And permeating the surrounding atmosphere is the smell of the gulls' guano.

The herring gulls arrive at the island in the spring from their open-water wintering areas along the coast. They come in search of secluded breeding grounds, and the remote lakes of the north woods provide ideal territories for their expanding population.

Not all gulls that search out this lake are herring gulls. In recent years another, rarer relative of these gulls has appeared each spring. On a nearby, flatter island, only a few feet above the midsummer's lake level, lives perhaps the most unusual island resident in the entire waterway, Bonaparte's gull (*Larus philadelphia*). This gull, petite and ternlike in appearance, is rarely known to breed south of an area stretching from Alaska to central Canada. But this remote, isolated island, situated near the edge of the boreal forest, offers an ideal home for this tree-nesting gull. White pine more than thirty feet high surrounded by spruce and northern white cedar shelter and camouflage the bird's twiggy nests, which are lined with grasses, mosses, and lichens. On the northern end of the island, the top of a tall white cedar serves as a lookout perch and is often used to launch an aggressive, swooping attack on intruders.

The islands are also popular sites for other birds. Overhead, sleek, fork-tailed terns often hover in the steady breezes.

A Bonaparte's gull leaves a lookout perch on its nesting island in Allagash Lake. This petite, ternlike gull rarely breeds this far south and east in North America.

And on a July day, one might see fledgling spotted sandpipers scampering on the rocks at the water's edge, ready to dart into the dense low vegetation growing on the islands.

THE OUTLET

Northward from the gull islands, up the densely wooded shoreline to the lake's outlet, the rocks make their mediating influence between forest and water more fully apparent, rising abruptly and steeply near the islands but emerging ramplike from the water near the outlet cove. Here, in a major flow, the glacier slid from the lake basin up over the hard slate.

Today the points of gray, beachlike ledges protruding along the lakeshore leave no doubt that they represent the glacier's signature. The line-etched, smoothed surfaces, which fronted the glacier, tell the story despite the dark, slippery algae that now coat the once polished rock. Some ledges feature lichen-"painted" sidewalls at right angles to the shoreline where the rock has broken along joint planes.

Between the rocky prominences, pocket beaches continue to collect fragments removed by the weathering action of freezing and thawing water. Unprotected from the pounding waves, which are regularly driven down the expanse of lake by westerly winds, the rocky fragments are tumbled and jostled by the surf until they are worn round and smooth. Here, among bleached pieces of washed-in driftwood, the square stems of marsh skullcap (*Scutellaria epilobiifolia*) push through the polished stones to color the sterile beaches with their green, minty leaves and pale violet-blue flowers.

On the shore north of the outlet, in marked contrast to the ledges of the opposite side, the currents and waves have left a cobble beach of smooth, rounded rocks like those in the small pocket beaches described above. The beach sweeps in a long, shallow arc to the stream exiting the lake. For thousands of years the winds pushed ice and water onto the beach, violently turning and grinding the rocks until they settled and fitted like a cobble street. Human hands, however, would be hard put to pave an area as interesting. Up close, the pink cast of the beach gives way to all shades of red, white, black, blue, and green. Veined and contoured sandstones, coarse conglomerates, darkly hued slates, siltstones with sandwiched veins of quartz, green volcanics pitted with tiny cavities, and banded gneiss cover the shore along with a final touch of molted bird feathers, mussel shells, and green tufts of grass.

Along these two markedly different shores the currents flow, draining the entire watershed above into the lower section of Allagash Stream.

Gravel bars in Allagash Stream support dense stands of tall, colorfully flowered plants, such as this large purple fringed orchis.

The Lower Stream

The stream comes out of Allagash Lake in two shallow, sandy channels, swirls around small islands, and begins a five-mile descent to Chamberlain Lake ninety-three feet below. Once free of the islands, it straightens out and drops quickly, taking on again the vigorous characteristics of a youthful stream—narrow, straight, fast, and boulder strewn. Overhanging cedars, spruce, pine, and yellow birch cast a deep shade over its channel. In an area of outcrops, the stream drops over a ledge, and near the pool below in a clearing, orange-yellow Canada lilies (*Lilium canadense*) brighten the streamside woods. Their spotted, bell-shaped flowers, supported on gracefully arched stems, nod in the slightest breeze. Butterflies have difficulty reaching the upside-down flowers, so they defer to bees and hummingbirds. Indians once used the fleshy roots of this plant to thicken soups and made a root tea for stomach sickness and rheumatism.

The stream moves on, occasionally passing trees pruned evenly several feet above the rapids and holding the debris of grass and driftwood—evidence of higher water, for no dam controls this flowage. Even a day's rain will bring a quick response in water level and flow rate. As the stream begins to flatten out, small grassy and weedy backwaters appear along its edges. Gravel bars increase, and on them the large purple fringed orchis (*Habenaria fimbriata*) grows—one of the waterway's most beautiful native orchids. Its one- to five-foot-tall, leafy stem supports a cylinder of lavender flowers at its top. The intricate flowers have oval sepals and finely toothed petals. A fringe ornaments the three fan-shaped lobes of the flower's lip petals. As with its relative, the white fringed orchis, a tubular, hollow spur points backward from the base of each flower. This part of the flower is sought out by moths in search of nectar. In true orchid fashion the flower is designed to ensure its pollination. When a moth extends its long tongue into the spur, its head encounters a sticky disk of pollen on one of the flower's anthers, which it then carries to another flower.

High, mucky banks border the stream as it approaches Little Round Pond. The crowns of speckled alder balloon out over the channel, competing for sunlight in the open space above the water. Dense stands of sensitive fern (*Onoclea sensibilis*) and grasses cover unstable areas swept by high waters. Swamp milkweed (*Asclepius incarnata*) pushes up through the cover of vegetation to sway in the breeze as high as four feet above the streambank. The milkweed's flat-topped cluster of flowers attracts many insects, sometimes to their demise. An intricate mechanism, designed to provide for the transportation of pollen from one flower to another via an insect's leg, doesn't always work. For example, when a honeybee (*Apis mellifera*) lands on one of the tiny quarter-inch flowers to drink nectar, the tarsal segments near the ends of its hind legs slip

A male ruby-throated hummingbird investigates a stand of Canada lilies growing in a small forest opening beside Allagash Stream. This tiny aerobatical bird has little difficulty in maneuvering to obtain nectar from these upside-down flowers.

into little slits in the sides of the flower. As the insect tries to extricate itself, filaments attached to tiny pollen bags catch on the tarsal segments and are carried to the next flower. Unfortunately, the leg is sometimes caught in one of the slits and the insect is trapped.

Humans should exercise caution, too, but for a different reason. Tea made from the roots of swamp milkweed was once used for asthma, rheumatism, and heart ailments, but it is now known to be potentially toxic.

Continuing downstream, the water deepens and the current slows. Forested banks on both sides lower to stream height and turn the stream into a corridor of alders—two runs of tangled shrubs thrusting out into Little Round Pond.

LITTLE ROUND POND

Almost immediately after the thick, shrubby banks let go of the quieted stream, one emerges suddenly and unexpectedly into the bright open space of a small body of water. Little Round Pond is shallow and muddy, and around it everything appears flat. The panorama of forest is low and evenly topped. Along the shoreline from northwest to south, northern white cedar dominate the spruce, fir, white pine, and tamarack. The edge between the water and the swampy land is further concealed by low lines of alders, shrubby heaths, marsh grasses, rushes, and sedges. A wide half-moon of wetland rests up against the west shore, fed by channels of a small brook. In summer, beautiful pink-red blossoms of northeastern rose and the bright yellow flowers of shrubby cinquefoil (*Potentilla fruticosa*) provide a backdrop for tall, dark red blossoms of pitcher plants and profuse stands of royal fern (*Osmunda regalis*) topped by fertile leaflets sporting clusters of spore cases.

Cold springs in the pond, plentiful food, and gravelly spawning areas in the stream above contribute to an abundance of brook trout. In this undisturbed environment, the laws of nature are relatively free to work. Common mergansers (*Mergus merganser*) pursue the pond's fish population. Loons also ply the waters for fish, and, if the opportunity presents itself, have been known to take a duckling for a meal. Any such overt move on the part of a loon or other predator will prompt a family of ducks to disperse rapidly, the young paddling furiously for the cover of vegetation at the water's edge while the parent decoys the assailant by circling and loudly flapping its wings and splashing.

Loons, it seems, also have another duck-pursuit strategy besides the open-water chase. A loon on this pond was once observed floating some distance from an apparently unconcerned family of black ducks swimming in open water. Upon aligning itself in the direction of the ducks, the loon slowly sank like a submarine and disappeared below the surface. Moments later it burst out of the water in the middle of the duck family, rearing up and flapping its wings vigorously. Ducks flew in all directions with the loon in pursuit—unsuccessful in this case.

While adult loons have little to fear from predators, their nests and young are often vulnerable. Loons nesting at the water's edge in undammed lakes and ponds, such as this where water levels are free to flood in response to spring melting or heavy rainfall, face the danger of high water inundating their nests. On one trip to Little Round Pond, this writer observed an abandoned nest with two unhatched eggs, one dislodged and lying in the water below the nest.

During summer evenings cow moose feed in the pond, leaving trails of bubbles, muddy water, and floating bits of chomped grass as they slosh just offshore along the marshy banks. Calves lie well hidden in the alders some distance away, alert to parental calls. Muskrats (*Ondatra zibethicus*) leave wakes near the shore and disappear at the mouths of weedy channels. Merganser families settle in at night behind screens of vegetation at the marsh's edge. Often the reddish coats of deer can be glimpsed beneath high, bushy alders on the forested shore.

The dense cedar swamp beyond the north shore of the pond is well browsed and hoof-trampled from many seasons of use by deer as a wintering area. The swamp is an exceptional deer "yard" in terms of the food and protection it provides to enable the deer to survive the hardships of winter. Unlike moose, which can lift their feet nearly shoulder high, deer are unable to lift their feet clear of snow more than six inches deep without dragging them along the surface. Thus, in deep snow, the deer are forced to congregate in yards where they can work together to trample a maze of paths to sources of food. Tips of white cedar and hemlock needles are some of their favorites. They also feed on the buds of maple (*Acer* spp.), dogwood (*Cornus* spp.), aspen (*Populus* spp.), and willow (*Salix* spp.). Gathering in yards allows deer to conserve energy, and they generally bed down here during the day, creating hollows of melted snow. As they rest and chew their cuds, their four-chambered ruminant digestive system enables them to digest even this tough winter browse.

Little Round Pond is actually a sixty-acre pool—a widening of the stream. But why has it occurred here? The answer is linked to the sound of rushing water coming from around a corner at the pond's outlet.

FALLS AND DROPS

The formation of Little Round Pond is the result of the same geologic events that produced the bedrock foundation of the islands and outlet ledges of the lake above. At the pond's outlet, upturned layers of resistant Seboomook Slate block the flow of the stream and back it up until the pond rises and overflows its natural dam. Then in a roaring, swirling rush, the stream steps down a total of twenty feet, contained by a misty, spray-soaked, rocky corridor lined with northern white cedar.

Shaped by thousands of years of erosion, Little Allagash Falls channels the stream over three drops. The first is shallow and broadly U-shaped, only two feet high, bordered on the north side by a low, flat, glacially scratched slate ledge.

Little Allagash Falls, at the outlet of Little Round Pond, channels Allagash Stream over three drops to a pool twenty feet below. It is listed on the Register of Maine's Critical Areas because it is an excellent example of resistant bedrock blocking the flow of water and forming a waterfall, and also because if its highly scenic natural setting.

Then the channel narrows and splits. The major chute makes a sudden, thunderous drop of fifteen feet through a cut in the slate. On the north side of the stream, a smaller, twisting channel siphons off some of the flow. At the base of the falls, a final three-foot-high ledge drop fans out the foaming water into a large, deep, boulder-strewn pool. The chemically "soft" water, darkened and acidified by the decaying vegetation in the pond and swamps above, gives a yellowish cast to the foamy rapids and pools.

During summer periods when the water is low, the rushing water is bordered by striated bedding planes eroded into relief and populated by tenacious clumps of bright green, moist moss, gray lichens, and lonely tufts of grass. Pools of water in finely ground and polished potholes of many sizes reflect the sky and sun. On the north side of the small left channel, the current continues to wear the open face of a giant pothole, part of its circular wall long since removed by the stream's erosive action. In winter all of this detail is completely covered by layers of ice.

Below the falls, the stream rests briefly in the deep, foam-specked pool, hemmed in on both sides by steep, forested banks. Then it quickly resumes its youthfully reckless journey.

Three ledge drops of one to two feet appear in quick succession, betraying the otherwise hidden influence of the gray slate on the stream's descent. Then the grade levels out and gravel bars once more begin to form. In summer the bars are colored with the reds, purples, yellows, and whites of swamp milkweed, large purple fringed orchis, swamp candles (*Lysimachia terrestris*), and tall meadow rue (*Thalictrum polygamum*). All exhibit the long-stemmed, flowering profusion of plants responding to abundant light and moisture in unstable environments.

The water becomes deeper and the current less perceptible. Overhanging dead trunks of trees line the evergreen banks. The stream is now more than four hundred feet lower than when it came out of seclusion in Allagash Pond some twenty miles to the northwest. The intimacy of the narrow stream disappears quickly and is soon replaced by the vast expanses of another feature of the northern wilderness—the large lakes.

At Little Allagash Falls, glacial scratches are visible on a worn ledge of Seboomook slate.

A pothole in the slate rocks at Little Allagash Falls shows the powerful grinding effect of stones and coarse sediments whirled in an eddy over thousands of years.

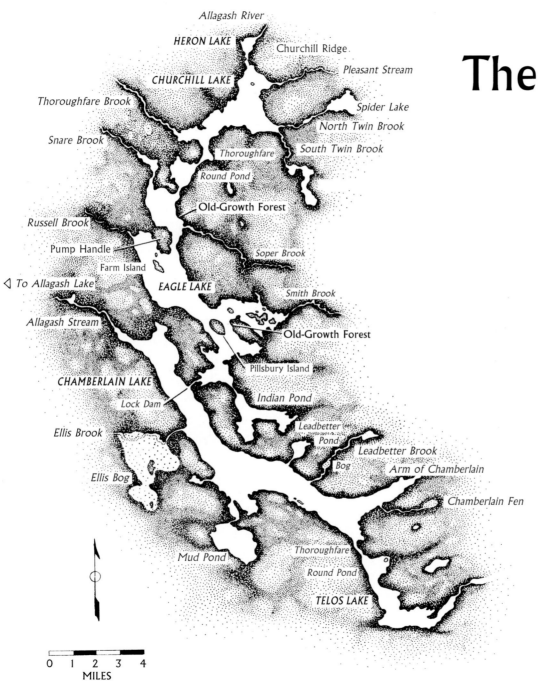

The Large Lakes

Allagash River

HERON LAKE

Churchill Ridge

CHURCHILL LAKE

Pleasant Stream

Thoroughfare Brook

Spider Lake

North Twin Brook

Snare Brook

South Twin Brook

Thoroughfare

Round Pond

Old-Growth Forest

Russell Brook

Soper Brook

Pump Handle

Farm Island

◁ To Allagash Lake

Smith Brook

EAGLE LAKE

Allagash Stream

Old-Growth Forest

Pillsbury Island

CHAMBERLAIN LAKE

Indian Pond

Lock Dam

Ellis Brook

Leadbetter Pond

Leadbetter Brook

Bog

Arm of Chamberlain

Ellis Bog

Chamberlain Fen

Thoroughfare

Mud Pond

Round Pond

TELOS LAKE

0 1 2 3 4
MILES

The lakes of the north woods are second in distinction only to the large tracts of forest. They dramatically introduce sights, sounds, and smells unknown to the woods. Their bright, airy spaciousness contrasts sharply with the dark, light-flecked, closed forest that spreads its roots to their shores.

The waterway encompasses four large interconnected lakes and several smaller bodies of water. Three—Chamberlain, Eagle, and Churchill—cover an area of more than twenty-two thousand acres, in excess of thirty-four square miles of surface water. The low surrounding land belies the depth of the lakes, two of which are more than one hundred feet deep. The result is an extensive storage capacity controlling the flow of the river downstream and stabilizing water levels for fish, loons, and other aquatic animal life.

The rocks and fossils in the Allagash lakes region suggest a restless history of land formation and movement.[1] Theories of plate tectonics place this part of Old North America near the equator, where it lay for 300 million years or more. During this time it experienced several major continental batterings with attendant periods of mountain building and faulting. At least three times it submerged in tropical seas and became a settling basin for sediments washed off the surrounding land. During these periods the remains of marine animals were entombed in the accumulating materials. On land, the subtropical primitive plants, restricted to the wetter parts of the landscape, couldn't have been more unlike the northern flora we see here today.

Sometime less than 200 million years ago, the continent began to move northward. As the land drifted to its present latitude, erosion took its inexorable toll, removing layer after layer of rock and cutting through the slates and other formations to reveal rocks of more ancient lineage. Today the lay of the land, the exposed outcrops, and the fossils all combine to give provocative hints of this unfinished story.

During more recent times the lake basins here were oriented and further defined by glaciation. The first glacial flows were strong, and because they moved parallel to some faults and other lines of fracture and perpendicular to the bedrock folds, significant erosion undoubtedly occurred.

When the ice left the lakes area, over eleven thousand years ago, the region was experiencing a pronounced environmental change and, quite likely, the arrival of humans. The climate was becoming warmer and wetter, and winter snowfall was increasing. These changes were due to the retreat of the ice sheet and its effects on the Gulf Stream, as well as to the shift in the drainage of the Great Lakes from the Mississippi to the St. Lawrence River.

Wildlife species were affected by the changing conditions. Mastodons and woolly mammoths, which may have lived in this region, became extinct. Other animals that may have roamed here and felt the effects of these major changes include the musk ox, grizzly bear, and North American horse.[2]

Revegetation occurred rather rapidly following deglaciation.[3] For possibly two or three hundred years, conditions were unstable without the cover of soil-holding plants. Large quantities of rock flour, ground in the glacial mill, washed into lakes and streams. As the ice receded and conditions warmed, tundra vegetation became established, followed by open woodlands and then a closed forest.

Throughout the centuries the composition of the forest varied, probably due to changes in climate, disease, and soil conditions. Hemlock, American beech, oak (*Quercus* spp.), white pine, and yellow birch all had their day. About fifteen hundred to a thousand years ago, a cooling climate spurred the increase of spruce and fir in the region. Today this northern forest, with its prevalence of cedar swamps and peatlands, still exists, but here around the lakes the spruce and fir are mixed with a greater abundance of northern hardwoods.

In these north woods probably the major reason the conifers were more successful than the hardwoods is their ability to grow on poor soils. They can get by with fewer mineral nutrients, and they are more frugal with those they do take in, particularly since they do not have to replace all their leaves every year.

After the last glacier left, the organic build-up of soil had to start on a barren landscape of bedrock and rock fragments, and at this latitude its making is slow. Cool conditions slow the breakdown of organic material, with the frequent result that little nitrogen is released. The consequence is a thickening of the mat of coniferous needles (called mor humus) on the forest floor. Further, with the high amount of precipitation in this region, available nutrients are subject to leaching and are lost from the topsoil. Moreover, the acidity of the conifer needles compounds the problem by increasing the soil's already acid condition, with its accompanying effect of "locking up" nutrients so that they are unavailable to plants.

In the lakes region of the waterway, the soils are stony and often composed of large percentages of silts and clays.[4] Depths range from shallow, around a foot deep or less on the tops of ridges and hills, to deep, up to five feet or more in the lowlands. But even where they are deep they are nutrient deficient and often poorly drained. Typically the soil is gray: a thin black layer of decomposed organic matter overrides a whitish gray layer from which nutrients have been leached by the downward percolation of acid water. This ashy, leached layer derived its name, spodsol, from the Russian word *podsol*, which means "ash earth."

Soil is a place of consumption, unlike the canopy, where production is the primary function. Here in the coniferous forest, fungi are more likely to be involved in the breakdown of organic matter than are bacteria. Mites (order Acarina) are also important, and many are specialized. One species lays its eggs inside fallen balsam fir needles so that its larvae can feed on them. Springtails (order Collembola), another kind of insect, are numerous in mor humus, being saprophages, or eaters of dead plant materials.

Where broad-leaved trees, such as aspen, have existed for some time, a gray-brown spodsol may be found. The layer of leaf litter in this kind of forest is known as mull humus and may not be as thick as that beneath the conifers. The soil in this case tends to be less acidic and richer in nutrients, with larger populations of bacteria and earthworms.

Thus the character of these north woods is the result of a complex combination of climate, geologic processes, and living things. For many reasons it is the latter that often promote the greatest interest in wild areas, and it is along the shores of the lakes that many species are most apt to reveal themselves. This is nowhere truer than in the lakes of the Allagash Waterway.

Early morning mists rise off the waters along
Chamberlain Lake's rocky northeastern shore.

Ancient fossils lie embedded in outcrops along the shores of the
Allagash. They tell of a time when this region was near the equator
and covered by warm tropical seas. This fossil coral lived more than
400 million years ago. The green leaves are northern white cedar.

Chamberlain Lake

Often the most interesting place to enter a wilderness lake is at its inlet end. This is where wildlife are frequently found, because inlets are usually shallow and marshy. Such conditions are created by the sediments carried in by rivers and streams and gently distributed on the lake's bottom by the slowing current. In a long-term view, inlets are the beginning of the end of lakes, where the gradual filling of a lake's basin actively begins. Such is the character of the inlet at the northwest end of Chamberlain Lake—the largest of the Allagash lakes.

The intimacy of Allagash Stream dissolves into a broad shallow cove, fringed in summer with a wide marshy shoreline punctuated by the bleaching stubs of lifeless tree trunks. Against the light greens and grays, the black, half-submerged hulks of feeding moose and the red, graceful forms of grazing deer quickly catch the eye. Occasionally a bit of blue-gray appears—a great blue heron pursuing its successful freeze-and-wait fishing strategy. In early morning, and again as evening approaches, the marsh comes alive with the sights and sounds of feeding animals. Trout rise and blurp bursts of ripples on the quiet surface, while overhead the tree swallows (*Iridoprocne bicolor*) swoop and chatter—both after the latest hatch of insects. Belted kingfishers (*Megaceryle alcyon*) rattle their presence on their way to a favorite fishing perch. From off in the woods the loud knocking of a pileated woodpecker (*Dryocopus pileatus*) echoes across the cove. Near the shore, bullfrogs harrumph and moose splash noisily in their submerged pastures.

Beyond the cove, the immensity of the lake reveals itself. It is not wide, ranging from less than a mile to a little over two miles, but it is long and straight—about fourteen miles, with an eastern arm a little more than three miles long. The shore is rocky, narrow, and often appears uninteresting. But there are hidden surprises, such as a small pocket beach concealed behind a slaty ledge that rises out of the water on the

A slaty ledge along the shore of Chamberlain Lake supports the bright orange lichen *Xanthoria elegans*. Above the lichen grow tufts of the rusty woodsia fern and a stand of red pine.

north shore. The ledge is topped with a beautiful stand of red pine, and below, its dark face is strikingly colored by the bright orange lichen *Xanthoria elegans*. Tufts of the small fern rusty woodsia (*Woodsia ilvensis*) sprout from clefts in the rock. With luck, a careful search of crevices might reveal the well-camouflaged once-married underwing moth. Partially submerged at the foot of the ledge sits an unorthodox beaver lodge wedged between broken rocks. A short walk down the shoreline uncovers further evidence of the beaver: chips and debarked limbs in among swamp smartweed (*Polygonum coccineum*), cut-leaved water horehound (*Lycopus americanus*),

The Katahdin range exerts an imposing presence over Chamberlain Lake.

and the ubiquitous woolgrass, (*Scirpus cyperinus*), that grows at the water's edge.

The outstanding view from the north shore—and, for that matter, from almost any location on the lake—is Mount Katahdin twenty-five miles to the southeast. Its mile-high peak and retinue of attendant mountains exert a constant presence over all the big lakes in the waterway. A sense of security is imparted by mountains in wild country. Perhaps it comes from feeling watched over or perhaps from the sense of their timelessness or even from the awareness of place that they prompt. From the lakes the Katahdin range appears vibrant and alive, reshaping itself to the clouds and their shadows and exhibiting a spectrum of pastel shades as it changes from one subtle hue to another in response to the atmosphere and light. But the sublime beauty of these northern lakes and their surroundings must be enjoyed in the moment, for one of the lessons here is that it is a fragile beauty subject to sudden change.

STORMS

Sensitive to the whims of weather, the big lakes are easily roused within minutes from their placidity to wild, wavetossed, rumpled sheets of water. Winds are frequent here, blowing mostly from westerly directions—north by northwest in winter and south by southwest in summer. They blow up quickly, sometimes to hurricane force.

In the summer, thunderstorm activity increases; fifteen to thirty occur

over the course of a year in this region. Dorothy Kidney, who lived on the shore of Chamberlain Lake at Lock Dam, gives a vivid description of the calamitous effects these electrical storms can have upon the lakes:

> *Never in my life have I seen thunderstorms such as we had at Lock Dam! The storms would come crashing down upon us, blasts of thunder would shake the forest, and at night lightning would turn our north country into daylight. The wind and lightning would snap trees off all around us, the lake would lash fiercely at the shore, and rain would threaten to pound everything right into the ground.[5]*

One hundred years earlier, Henry Thoreau huddled in his tent a few miles away writing of a similar experience:

> *We listened to some of the grandest thunder which I had ever heard,—rapid peals, round and plump, bang, bang, bang, in succession, like artillery from some fortress in the sky; and the lightning was proportionately brilliant. The Indian said, "It must be good powder." All for the benefit of the moose and us, echoing far over the concealed lakes. I thought it must be a place which thunder loved, where the lightning practised to keep its hand in, and it would do no harm to shatter a few pines.[6]*

ANCIENT RELICTS

The shoreline of the lake is rocky, in some sections shallow, dropping off steeply in others. On sunny days when the lake is calm, huge boulders can be seen through the clear water. Along some parts of the shore, rock outcrops appear; and at the southeastern end of the lake, small rocky islands protrude from the water, several along the southern shore. Waves, sweeping down the length of the lake, are high at this end and vigorously maintain the barren nature of the outcrops. Here one can read more than 500 million years of history.

The oldest rocks beneath the forests and lakes are composed of sediments thought to have been laid down some 500 million years ago during Cambrian times. They were once a half-mile thick, and during the next 100 million years were covered by additional sediments to a depth of perhaps as much as eight miles. Today these ancient sediments appear as metamorphosed rocks of phyllite and slate. They can be found on the north shore of the lake near its eastern end and down the shore of the Arm of Chamberlain. The formation surfaces again opposite the Arm just east of the largest island along the south shore.

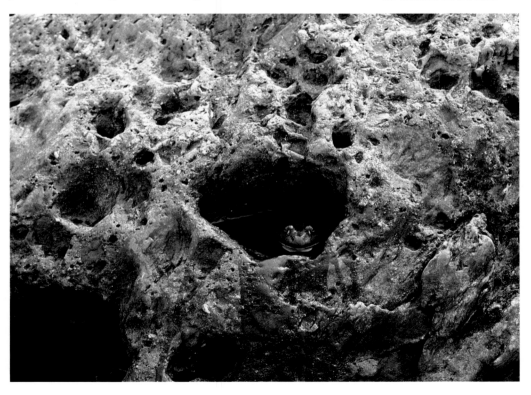

A fossil-studded conglomerate outcrop on the southeastern shore of Chamberlain Lake often hosts frogs in the pools of rainwater collected in its weathered surface.

Also on the shore opposite the Arm, at the east end of a ledge point and again on an island a little less than a mile to the west, the fossilized remains of ancient life lie imbedded in 400-million-year-old conglomerate. These include traces of variously shaped corals—fans, cylinders, chains, honeycombs, horns—and remnants of extinct spongelike animals called stromatoporoids, all of which grew in warm, tropical seas. Some of the fossils are visible in the numerous holes that pock the conglomeratic outcrop as a result of thousands of years of wave-induced erosion. The fossils, however, aren't the exclusive inhabitants of these cavities, for in those which have collected water, frogs contentedly sit, secure in their private domiciles.

LAKE LIFE

As in ancient times, water is still the great attractor of life, but Chamberlain Lake is a marked departure from the warm seas that once covered the area. Now the waters are fresh and much cooler. The lake is oligotrophic, as are most lakes in the waterway: cold, clear, well oxygenated, and deep—up to 154 feet. The clarity of the water allows greater penetration of light; consequently, photosynthesis by minute phytoplankton such as algae can occur at greater depths. At times, perhaps several times a year, the food-producing algae bloom in great numbers, providing sustenance for such zooplankton as rotifers (phylum Rotifer), water fleas, and copepods (subclass Copepoda). These animals, unlike the photosynthesizers, are not necessarily held to the sunlit areas near the lake's surface but may move down to greater depths. Being thus distributed over a wide area in the lake, they are available to satisfy the hunger of a variety of aquatic animals, including the fry of trout, which begin their lives feeding on plankton.

It is therefore not surprising that the lake is ideal habitat for lake and brook trout. The lake whitefish is also plenti-ful. This fish is fairly deep through the middle, with a small, pointed head and small mouth. It averages sixteen to twenty inches in length and weighs two to five pounds. Most of its hunting is done on the bottom. Other fish include the horn-pout (*Ictalurus nebulosus*), round whitefish, white sucker, long-nose sucker, and cusk, or burbot. The burbot is unusual look-ing: a long, eellike body, olive-brown and splotchy above, with long dorsal and ventral fins and a single chin barbel project-ing from its lower jaw. Generally it feeds on the bottom, espe-cially during the summer months, but during colder seasons it feeds throughout the lake, preying on smaller fish.

The abundance of fish also attracts herring gulls and loons. The gulls inhabit a small rocky island about three-quar-ters of a mile off the north shore near a small stream drain-ing Leadbetter Pond. Interestingly, their arrival here each spring appears to be timed at about thirty days after the ice goes out.

Loons are also plentiful around the lake, especially favor-ing the fishing grounds along the protected south and south-west shore in the lee of the prevailing winds. They are often seen feeding their young in the small entrance to the cove into which the Mud Pond brook empties. It was near here in 1857 that Thoreau stumbled out onto the lakeshore after getting lost on Mud Pond Carry—a portage route from the West Branch of the Penobscot's watershed to the Allagash's. Sleep-ing on the shore that night, he wrote: "We heard the voice of the loon, loud and distinct, from far over the lake. It is a very wild sound, quite in keeping with the place and circumstances of the traveler, and very unlike the voice of a bird. I could lay awake for hours listening to it, it is so thrilling."[7]

The loon's wild, unearthly calls still echo over the lake, but most travelers today will never see or hear some of the wild animals of Thoreau's day. One such animal is the wood-land caribou (*Rangifer tarandus*).

A common loon sits on its nest at the water's edge. Males and females have identical plumage, and both adults incubate the eggs. A typical clutch is two eggs, and incubation lasts almost a month.

THE GREAT RUNNER

Joe Polis, Thoreau's guide, called the caribou the great runner, probably because of the animal's extensive wandering. In those days it was a well-known inhabitant of these north woods. Even in the latter part of the nineteenth century the caribou was frequently sighted. One report came from the adventurer and writer Thomas Sedgwick Steele, who entered Chamberlain Lake through the Mud Pond Carry route around 1880. After crossing Mud Pond, a thin sheet of water only inches deep and covering a soft bottom of deep mud, he and his party came down the small brook draining into the cove of the lake. There, he wrote, "we were suddenly startled by hearing a loud splash in the water, and greeted with the vision of an immense bull caribou, which sprang up and instantly disappeared in the wood."[8]

A young woodland caribou as it appeared on the north shore of Chamberlain Lake in the spring of 1990. Native caribou have been absent from the waterway for nearly one hundred years. This caribou was one of the last to be released in Maine's north woods by the Maine Caribou Project. Based on a photograph taken by Allagash ranger Jim Kelly.

Indeed, these stocky animals must have been an impressive sight, for some bulls reached a weight of four to six hundred pounds. Although most females also sport antlers, the male's are much larger—up to five feet long with a five-foot spread. In addition, one or two broad, flat brow tines extend out vertically over the forehead nearly to the nose, presenting a formidable-looking piece of armor. Undoubtedly Steele, who ventured into the area in late summer, viewed the caribou's antlers while they were in velvet.

The caribou is well suited to water, having long, coarse, hollow guard hairs that help it to float. The fur also provides excellent insulation for the animal in winter. Although the caribou varies in color, it is generally brown with a yellow-white neck and mane and a whitish belly, rump, and legs. In summer the pads of its large, rounded hooves are large and soft, but in winter they shrink and harden, developing a rim that can bite into icy surfaces and prevent slipping.

Until the early 1900s, native woodland caribou were hunted in northern Maine and throughout the north woods from Alaska to Newfoundland. The commissioner of the Maine Department of Inland Fisheries and Game reported in 1886 that caribou were plentiful in Maine, but by most accounts they were gone shortly after the turn of the century. Lou Dietz, in his book *The Allagash*, suggested that the last caribou in the Allagash might have been the one killed in 1899 near the Michaud Farm on the lower Allagash River.[9] Another source placed the last legally shot caribou near Chase Rapids on the Allagash River in 1898.[10]

In the 1960s and again in the 1980s, efforts were undertaken to reintroduce the caribou into Maine. Both attempts were unsuccessful. But the last reintroduction effort did provide the rare opportunity for a few people to see a caribou on the shore of Chamberlain Lake, an event reminiscent of their presence here in an earlier time. Today this large deer of the north woods resides mostly in latitudes above the contiguous United States.

WINTER WOODS

Although the caribou may never again "float" over the Allagash snow on their oversized feet, it's certainly not due to a lack of the white cover, which is often present during eight months of the year. As the days shorten and the sun's rays strike the earth less directly, the temperature drops and the snows come ever more frequently. The snowpack deepens and a quiet settles over the forest. Wind becomes the major source of sound as it dries the woods and lowers the temperature. On severely cold nights the pop of freezing trees breaks the silence of the forest, and the lakes rumble as the ice shifts and cracks under the stress of expansion. Storms occur frequently, placing new burdens on overloaded branches. The effectively shaped spires of spruce and fir leave little opportunity for the weight of snow to break their tops. Branches bend easily under the weight, pointing their snow-covered fingers toward the accumulating snowpack below.

The woods become virtually soundproofed by the snow-covered trees. When the sun breaks through, a sparkling beauty transforms the forest into a fairytale land of strange shapes and mysterious shadows. Prisms of ice glitter colors of the rainbow. The clutter on the forest floor is now concealed beneath a many-layered, contoured blanket, sculpted and smoothed by the wind. Streams lie hidden and soundless; only dips in the snow cover and protruding vegetation suggest their presence. Silence, however, should not be mistaken for inactivity, for each day brings new physical changes, and life responds in ways directed by an innate drive to survive. Above the winter's deep snowpack, when days are warm, the evergreen conifers crank up their photosynthetic machinery into low-level production, as do the aspens in their chlorophyll-laden, green-

ish yellow bark. For the most part, however, the winter nuances of the forest's processes, compared with the survival activities of its animals, pass unnoticed.

The aspen's buds, grown when food-making activities were in full swing, now attract the ruffed grouse. And so it is with the pines, spruces, and firs, whose buds are food for the

Allagash Stream below Little Allagash Falls is sometimes barely visible beneath the ice and snow of winter.

spruce grouse, now sporting extra scales on its feet to better grip the icy branches. Below the forest cover, deer are now constrained to move along communally packed trails, browsing the coniferous leaves and deciduous buds. If ever they could be envious of their high-stepping relative, the moose, now is the time.

The winter strategies of other animals are now fully implemented. The snowshoe hare criss-crosses the soft carpet of snow camouflaged by its white coat of hairs, which are hollow to help conserve critically needed heat and energy. Coyotes and red foxes (*Vulpes fulva*) also leave their hunting patterns traced in the snow, but when they are not active they sleep curled up to decrease exposed surface area. Like many mammals, they are protected by thicker coats of fur. So, too, are deer and mice, whose fur insulation has now increased by a third. By erecting the hairs of their coats, these and the other mammals can gain even more insulative value.

Some animals rely on insulated nests to withstand the rigors of winter. Red squirrels have theirs in treetops or in holes in trees. Raccoons (*Procyon lotor*), too, hole up in tree dens, although they will also use underground holes. Trees are also homes of bark beetles (family Scolytidae), which winter over as larvae, pupae, or adults. Most insects are tucked away out of sight during the winter, but there is a noticeable exception; on warm days populations of springtails may emerge and by their sheer numbers blacken the snow at the bases of trees. Beetles, ants (family Formicidae), and other insects concealed in bark and wood of trees are much sought after by woodpeckers, especially the hairy (*Picoides villosus*) and pileated species—both common residents here. Their drumming is often heard for long distances, abruptly breaking the silence of the woods. Like black-capped chickadees (*Parus atricapillus*) sometimes do, they seek out individual cavities for resting on winter nights. Purple finches (*Carpodacus purpureus*) and blue jays (*Cyanocitta cristata*), on the other hand, roost among dense stands of conifers for protection.

There are other ways of coping, too. The black-capped chickadee is able to bring its body temperature as low as ten degrees centigrade, thus conserving 20 percent of its energy. Sometimes when foraging for food it joins the red-breasted nuthatch (*Sitta canadensis*) to make up small flocks, possibly as a way of detecting predators more readily and discovering more sources of food. Some bird species, however, such as the great blue heron and the eastern kingbird (*Tyrannus tyrannus*), solve their winter food problem by migrating to warmer climates.

The black-capped chickadee is a common year-round resident in the north woods. In winter chickadees usually travel in small flocks, flitting about the trees in search of food.

There is in these north woods a winter life beneath the snow as well as above. At the base of the snowpack the conversion of ice to water vapor creates a space of loose ice crystals called the subnivean environment. Here, insulated by the snow cover, short-tailed shrews (*Blarina brevicauda*) and deer mice remain active. And where light penetrates, some evergreen plants, including the Christmas fern (*Polystichum acrostichoides*), still carry on limited photosynthesis.

Many plants and animals survive winter beneath ground level. Many perennials have corms or roots that can regenerate themselves. Annuals overwinter as seeds. Deer mice congregate in nests and keep warm by huddling together. Similarly, bees and ants keep warm in colonies numbering into the thousands. Toads bury themselves as much as three feet deep in soft soil by digging with their hind feet. Wood frogs, in contrast, only bury themselves a few inches deep. They are capable of freezing solid and surviving; their cells are protected from freezing inside by large amounts of concentrated sugar, while the water outside the cells is allowed to freeze.

A number of mammals den up for winter, the black bear being the largest. Not a true hibernator, it drifts in and out of deep sleep. The mink (*Mustela vison*) and the river otter (*Lutra canadensis*) are active mammals. They occupy dens, too, but venture out in search of food. The few snake species in this area survive by hibernating in old burrows and other holes.

Along the exposed streams, stone flies and caddis flies may mate during warm days in February. Black flies may also make an appearance on the snow-covered shores, although they tend to overwinter as active larvae along with mayflies and midges (family Chironomidae).

Life also survives beneath the ice of lakes and ponds. In some places where light penetrates the ice and snow, the waterweed *elodea* continues to photosynthesize and grow. Fish, muskrats, and beaver are active, along with back swimmers, and water boatmen. But for the summer inhabitants of the surface film or those that live just beneath it, the effects of winter ice have called for completely new living strategies. Scales of duckweed (family Lemnaceae) settle to the bottom and wait until after the spring ice-out, when they can float to the top and repopulate the surface. Water striders hibernate as adults in and under plant debris near the water's edge. Whirligig beetles and mosquito larvae live out the winter in the bottom mud along with dragonflies, damselflies, leeches (class Hirudinea), mussels, frogs, and turtles. Here also lie the roots of cattails, reedgrass, and bulrushes, waiting for the warmth of spring.

BOGS AND FENS

Those aquatic plants which quietly wait out the winter beneath the lakes and ponds of the north woods also have a powerful role in the demise of their own environment. One has only to look at Mud Pond, on the south side of Chamberlain Lake, to see this. Clogged with aquatic vegetation to within inches of its surface, its fate is presaged by the many wetlands in this region. Some of these are bogs, which contain acid waters, have little flow, and receive their nutrients primarily from the atmosphere.[11] Others are more accurately called fens, a type of wetland that is nourished by nutrients from ground and surface water that often moves down a slight slope. The mineral-enriched waters promote a diversity of plant species.

Some fens develop a pattern of long parallel pools, called flarks, oriented at right angles to the flow of the wetland's waters. This is a phenomenon found among northern peatlands and is not completely understood. The overall impression, however, is of a ribbed pattern of pools interspersed with strings or ridges of vegetation.

An example of a patterned, or ribbed, fen lies eight miles directly east of Mud Pond and only a mile southeast of the tip of the Arm of Chamberlain. Known as Chamberlain Fen, this small wetland of twenty-six acres is one of about fifty ribbed fens in Maine.[12] This type of peatland is one of the unique features of the boreal and subarctic regions of northern North America.

Characteristically the fen slopes gently, in this case from east to west. Moose trails and the scat of moose, deer, and bear around the edge of the fen suggest that the area is well used by wildlife. Common snipe (*Capella gallinago*) and spruce grouse also visit. Other birds include the secretive Lincoln's sparrow (*Melospiza lincolnii*); the perch-singing swamp sparrow (*Melospiza georgiana*); the tree swallow, with its darting and swooping flight pattern; the thicket-hunting Nashville warbler (*Vermivora ruficapilla*); and the teetering northern waterthrush (*Seiurus noveboracensis*).

A typical moat, or wet lagg zone, surrounds the fen, where tamarack and speckled alder dominate along with northern white cedar. Beneath the trees the tall fronds of royal fern and cinnamon fern (*Osmunda cinnamomea*) sway in the breezes, accompanied by blue flag and stunted bog sedge (*Carex paupercula*). Ribbing occurs in the western half of the fen but is weakly developed. The interior of the fen contains about twenty discernible ribs, or strings, of vegetation. The most prominent rib is about a foot high. The mineral-rich waters provide conditions for a richly varied flora. Sphagnum mosses are the major plants of which the ribs are made, but they are also populated by mud sedge (*Carex limosa*), few-flowered sedge (*Carex pauciflora*), bog rosemary, pitcher plant, round-leaved sundew (*Drosera rotundifolia*), cottongrass, tamarack, and black spruce.

In the eastern half of the fen there are slightly raised areas containing sphagnum and sedge lawns, broken by hummocks. The drier lawns are homes for bog rosemary, leatherleaf, sheep laurel, black chokeberry (*Pyrus melanocarpa*), and black spruce. In wetter parts of the lawns there are extensive carpets of mud

sedge and *Sphagnum papillosum*—a robust, fat, light brown sphagnum moss. A close inspection of the hummocks reveals a colorful stratification of sphagnum species—the yellow-green *Sphagnum angustifolium* in the hollows, over which lies the red *S. magellanicum*, and on top the brown *S. fuscum*.

Depending on their wetness, the flarks, or pools, contain a variety of plants as well, including clumps of beakrushes (*Rhychospora alba*), rushes of the genus *Juncus*, bog bean (*Menyanthes trifoliata*), horned bladderwort, sphagnum mosses, sedges, three-leaved false Solomon's-seal (*Smilacina trifolia*), and yellow-eyed grass (*Xyris montana*). Muddy areas reveal the uncommon bog club moss (*Lycopodium inundatum*), a small, creeping moss with arching, bushy-topped fronds.

Other interesting plants include calopogon and rose pogonia orchids and a moss with the scientific name *Splachnum ampullaceum*. This odd-looking moss grows on moose dung. It is less than one inch high, and in its unripe stage it has lilac or purplish capsules, each with a slender upper portion and a swollen lower portion tapered at the bottom.

Wetlands, such as this one near Chamberlain Lake, exist
throughout the waterway. They are home to many unusual
plants and attract a variety of wildlife species.

Round Pond and Telos Lake

These red pines on the north shore of Telos Lake are near the spot Henry David Thoreau described when he stopped to observe a stand of these trees in 1857.

Two miles west and south of the small brook that drains Chamberlain Fen into the Arm of Chamberlain, the lake narrows into a small thoroughfare that leads southeast to Round Pond—a body of water approximately a mile in diameter. A small island of Seboomook slate in a cove along the pond's northern shore reveals the fossilized skeletal remains of early Devonian crinoids. These once beautifully colored, flowerlike animals, called sea lilies, grew in colonies in ancient oceans. Their fossils are often found with those of two species of *Platyceras*. These gastropods lived in coiled, cone-shaped shells and had a rather unusual association with the crinoid: they attached themselves to the crinoid's anus and lived on its feces. Thus *Platyceras*, early pioneers in waste recycling, were able to help take care of the crinoid's sanitary housekeeping.

Round Pond narrows at its south end and then opens into Telos Lake. Both bodies of water offer spectacular views of Mount Katahdin. Along the northern shore of Telos Lake, rocky points of slate protrude. It was here that Thoreau stopped to look at some red pines, the first he had noticed on his trip in 1857. Red pine undoubtedly grows along this shore because it is sunny and the land is dry and rocky. The shore itself is home for a variety of plants, including marsh speedwell (*Veronica scutellata*), a spearwort (*Ranunculus* sp.), wild mint (*Mentha arvensis*), water parsnip (*Sium suave*), and lance-leaved goldenrod (*Solidago graminifolia*).

In the third cove west of the largest point on this shore another collection of fossils speaks of the ancient history of the land. Bivalved mollusks and spiral-shelled gastropods once lived here. The site also has yielded the fossils of trilobites—well-known extinct marine arthropods that scavenged the ocean bottom.

The northeasterly end of the lake narrows into a long valley that leads to a dam and, just beyond, the canal known as Telos Cut. Here, in the 1840s, the waters were made to flow through a gorge that possibly was once Telos Lake's ancient outlet. So today part of the Allagash waters flow south into the watershed of the East Branch of the Penobscot River, diverted from their original flow into Eagle Lake at what is now Lock Dam, an earthen structure on Chamberlain Lake.

Eagle Lake

The waters of Chamberlain Lake flow in a relative trickle through a conduit in Lock Dam. The brook-sized stream drops about fifteen feet in the half mile or more to Eagle Lake. On its way it flows over some of the waterway's oldest rocks—metamorphosed sedimentary rock more than 500 million years old. At the foot the stream slows as it opens into a broad marsh where uprooted, bleached skeletons of trees border the widening channel. Summer brings the dark shapes of feeding moose to mingle with the dead trunks and broken limbs. In the distance, between forested shores, the southern end of Eagle Lake's open water is visible. This is the most remote of the large lakes.

The lake's irregular shoreline conceals the inlets of brooks and streams where scoured outcrops shine and beaches smooth and straighten the shore's rough line. Islands and juts of land provide haven for wildlife and situations favoring old-growth trees. The lake itself, at 124 feet deep, is the home of burbot, trout, and whitefish.

ISLANDS

The southern entrance to the lake presents myriad coves and small islands. Pillsbury Island, the largest, a forested, egg-shaped hump not quite a mile long and half as wide, stretches across the end of the lake. A mixed growth of conifers and deciduous trees provides cover for a healthy deer population. Springs bubble from the ground near the northwest point of the island.

It was here that Thoreau stopped and waited out a thunderstorm—his farthest excursion north in the waterway. He explored the island's broad, rocky west shore and recorded the plants: willows, a member of the crowfoot, or buttercup, family Ranunculaceae, rough cinquefoil (*Potentilla norvegica*), mad-dog skullcap (*Scutellaria lateriflora*), asters (*Aster* spp.), a species of mint (family Labiatae), fireweed (*Epilobium angusti-folium*), a goldenrod (*Solidago* sp.), meadowsweet (*Spiracea lat-ifolia*), pussytoes (*Antennaria* sp.), self-heal (*Prunella vulgaris*), sheep sorrel (*Rumex acetosella*), raspberry (*Rubus* sp.), and woolgrass. He also noted that paper birch and quaking aspen (*Populus tremuloides*) were nearby.

North of Pillsbury Island, halfway down the west shore, a string of rocky nubbles and one large island strike northward.

Eagle Lake is the most remote of the large Allagash Lakes. In 1857 Henry David Thoreau entered the lake here at the south end through Lock Dam and canoed to Pillsbury Island, seen in the distance. To the right, across from the island, an old-growth forest contains pines that were alive when Thoreau made his trip.

The forested slope of Farm Island rises in a northerly direction to drop off in steep cliffs. The islands in the northern part of the string beyond Farm Island are low and rocky and sparsely vegetated with low shrubs, weather-beaten trees, persistent blueberries, and crevice-seeking pale corydalises (*Corydalis sempervirens*). Occasionally nesting loons single out low, rocky shelves on these innocuous-looking lakebound outcrops.

From a high ridge on the Pump Handle Peninsula, one can get a bird's-eye view of Eagle Lake and Farm Island.

OLD FORESTS

Opposite the southeast shore of Pillsbury Island, on a 400-million-year-old ridge of volcanic rock, stands an ancient forest of stalwart eastern white pine. Long, heavy horizontal branches give the tops an irregular, ragged, and flattened appearance. Interestingly, these conifers may be linked to a prehistoric ancestor that was living nearby during the very time when the bedrock on which these pines grow was formed.

It was in 1968, thirty miles to the southeast in the shadow of Mount Katahdin, that the fossil remains of an unusual primitive plant were first discovered.[13] Named *Pertica quadrifaria*, it was the tallest plant on the landscape 390 million years ago, even though its maximum height was only about six feet. However, unlike the pine on this ridge, *Pertica* had no leaves. Only its green, forked branches, curling up its one-inch-diameter stem in four spiraling rows, could manufacture its food. In fact, 390 million years ago leaves had not yet evolved.

Today, like its primitive ancestor, the white pine is the tallest living thing on the northeastern North American landscape. However, the pine's station in the north woods is not

what it once was. Its heyday came between ten thousand and seven thousand years ago in response to a general warming trend. Now it is relegated to associate status with respect to the major conifers of the boreal forest—the firs and spruces—making but shallow incursions into the southern edge of the swath of northern evergreens occupying the continent.

The Eagle Lake old-growth forest contains pine more than three feet in diameter and up to 130 feet tall—among the tallest in Maine.[14] Many were growing here when Thoreau passed by in 1857. In fact, some may have started their lives in the late 1700s. With a life span of up to 450 years, some may exist here for another two centuries or more provided that wind-throw, fire, or some other natural catastrophe does not occur. Ironically, one of these events may have been responsible for the pines becoming established on this ridge in the first place.

The white pine is a light-loving tree—in ecologist's language, the tree is intolerant to shade. When an opening is formed in the forest canopy—by storm damage, for example—pine has an opportunity to become established. Of course, other conditions must be right. Here on this ridge, the well-drained soil favors white pine. So, probably, did the slope. It is known, for example, that young trees along the steep-sided edges of watercourses receive more sunlight and thus are able to compete with aspens and maples, which on flatter landscapes can quickly overtop the pines and suppress their growth.

Beneath the broad canopy provided by these giants, the understory consists of scattered balsam fir, eastern hemlock, northern white cedar, red spruce, and sugar maple. Several of these are large and old in their own right. The ground level is dominated by twinflower, Canada mayflower (*Maianthemum canadense*), common wood-sorrel (*Oxalis montana*), bunchberry (*Cornus canadensis*), creeping snowberry (*Gaultheria hispidula*), and starflower (*Trientalis borealis*). But there are no

white pine seedlings, for so little light penetrates that they cannot compete and survive on the forest floor. Instead, seedlings of the shade-tolerant spruce and fir stand ready to make their debut as the leading characters.

The interior of this old forest is protected against the extremes of climate. The canopy and trees of the understory shield the ground-level environment from sun and wind. Here it is wetter and cooler than in exposed areas during the heat of the day, and because the canopy holds in heat, it is warmer at night. The lake's proximity helps in this respect, too. Lichens are prevalent, as are the mosses, such as the *Sphagnum* species in wet areas that store water and help maintain the humidity. Fungi grow throughout the soil beneath the forest floor, assisting the tree roots in capturing nutrients, aiding decomposition, and providing food for animals.

While this forest is not particularly rich in fauna, the animals, as in all habitats, can be categorized by what and where they eat. In summer up in the treetops, the red squirrels cut down the ripe pine cones, which drop to the ground where they can be expertly opened for their seeds. Other mammals include deer mice and shrews, which roam the forest floor; the pine marten (*Martes americana*), which hunts throughout the forest; and deer and moose, which seek shelter or just pass through.

Insect-eating warblers occupy many levels in the forest. The Cape May warbler (*Dendroica tigrina*) nests and hunts in the tops of the trees, while the bay-breasted warbler (*Dendroica castanea*) is attracted to the middle levels, especially near the tree trunks. And in the lower levels, the blackburnian warbler (*Dendroica fusca*) and magnolia warbler (*Dendroica magnoloia*) are often found. The black-throated green warbler (*Dendroica virens*) is also attracted to this forest, as is the golden-crowned kinglet (*Regulus satrapa*), which feeds high among the thick branches.

The most spectacular bird to inhabit this old-growth forest is the bald eagle. The pair living here are among the north-

A deer mouse peers over a mossy log on the forest floor. In the Northeast, this small rodent prefers forests of conifers and northern hardwoods, where it feeds on seeds, berries, mushrooms, worms and insects. Primarily nocturnal, it is active throughout the year.

ernmost nesting eagles in Maine. Their nest is a huge mass of sticks concealed beneath the uppermost branches of a large white pine. In true eagle fashion, however, the nest isn't used every year, as the eagles have more than one nest near this lake.

Six miles up the lake, on the north side of the outlet of Soper Brook, another stand of old-growth white pine towers above the forested shoreline.[15] This grove covers about eight acres, and the understory is composed of sugar maple, white birch, northern white cedar, and red spruce. One of the sugar maples is estimated to be 170 years old. The pine are thought to be younger, but they are of good size, ranging from twenty-five to thirty-one inches in diameter at breast height. Because of the density of the pine overstory, there are few ground-cover plants.

Across the lake, opposite the mouth of Soper Brook, is a pronounced peninsula called the Pump Handle. Here, on a high ridge some 150 feet above the lake, a three-acre stand of old-growth sugar maple and American beech is entering its second century. The ridge's mull soil—a loose, brown-colored, stony, clay loam—supports a ground-level story of beech and maple seedlings, beneath which grow trillium (*Trillium* sp.) and woodfern (*Dryopteris* sp.). A few red oaks also grow among the maples and beeches. The largest maple is thirty inches in diameter and sixty-five feet high.

The top of the Pump Handle's west ridge opens to moss-covered ledges and scattered evergreens and offers a scenic overlook of the lake. Laid out below are the islands, and on the western horizon ten miles away Allagash Mountain can be seen. Most interesting, however, is the lake's shoreline. Viewed from the lake surface, the shoreline appears smooth, the coves and points undiscernable, but from above its irregular pattern is revealed, especially the inlet coves of the brooks. Like the other lakes in this region of low topography and abundant water, Eagle Lake has many such small streams.

BROOKS

Troughs of folded Devonian rock channel two major brooks—Smith and Soper—into Eagle Lake on its eastern shore. Near Pillsbury Island the various channels of Smith Brook join to form the lake's largest cove, which is also one of its most beautiful. After his canoe trip here in the late 1800s, Thomas Sedgwick Steele was moved to write, "This sheet of water . . . presents most picturesque beauties in its windings as far as Haymoak [Haymock] Falls."[16]

After the high waters of spring subside, the outlet of Smith Brook becomes shallow but still retains enough water to cover its meandering channel. The low water is responsible for the beautiful color zones that appear along the shore on a clear summer day—deep blue waters roughly edged by gray-bleached dry-ki, followed by a band of light green grasses, and backed by the darker green of the forest. So thick and wide is the dry-ki, the jumble of dead trees, branches, and stumps, that it actually fences the stream. Thoreau wrote of encountering a barrier such as this when he attempted a safe landing while battling waves on Chamberlain Lake: "For half a dozen rods in width it was a perfect maze of submerged trees, all dead and bare and bleaching, some half their original height; others prostrate, and criss-across, above or beneath the surface, and mingled with them were loose trees and limbs and stumps, beating about."[17]

At its mouth the brook has left a low, sandy spit, now covered with pine. Back in the woods, northern white violet (*Viola pallens*) lights the forest floor, while the shore is brightened by the striking yellow of swamp candles, also known as yellow loosestrife. The shallow waters around this small, sandy point produce a zone of emergent plants—grasses, sedges, reeds, and clumps of bullhead lilies (*Nuphar variegatum*). Blue damselflies zigzag among them.

In the evening the mouth of the brook fills with the

sounds of wilderness: feeding moose snort and shake to clear their nostrils and ears, nervous deer blow at unseen disturbances, ducks burst out quacking, two loons converse in mournful tones, barred owls (*Strix varia*) begin their evening's hooting, osprey cheep high overhead, a light breeze sets the waves rhythmically lapping the shore and the pines soughing, thunder rumbles in the distance as lightning faintly flashes on the horizon.

The brook's long winding cove is a busy place almost any time of the day. Here the business of browsing and hunting seems to be always fully under way. Ospreys, herring gulls, and belted kingfishers maintain a busy air space overhead. Mergansers and black ducks seek their respective food sources—fish in the first case and aquatic plants in the second. Several loons occasionally congregate for reasons known only to themselves. Muskrats leave purposeful wakes along the weedy shore. Here, in the shallows among the dry-ki, spotted sandpipers and great blue herons hunt, each in their characteristic manner, the hyperactive sandpipers nervously running and picking about while the conservative herons rely on stealth.

Smith Brook is a great attraction for deer and moose. Vegetation is lush along the shore, and the shallows support a profusion of aquatic plants. Secluded coves and backwaters are numerous, and at times each appears to have its own resident bull moose. The deer feed close to shore, often hidden behind the dry-ki among the shrubs and the summer's crop of tall grasses, only the velvet-covered antlers of the bucks protruding above the vegetation.

In the 1800s the deer were not as plentiful along this waterway. The grasses and hardwood saplings and

A bull moose emerges onto Russell Brook Beach.

buds they favored were not abundant in the undisturbed spruce-fir forest, except in areas where fire, insects, disease, or wind-throw opened the woods to new growth. But the coming of the ax in this northern forest brought with it not only more deer but the dry-ki along the lake shores. Clearings in the forest are promoting the growth of favored deer browse, and in the past, dams built to control the river flow for log drives flooded trees along shorelines and brought about their demise.

Deer are still sought by many predators in this north country, but there was one predator in the history of this waterway that looked upon the deer as a special delicacy—the mountain lion (*Felis concolor*). Although this great cat probably was always rare here, there is enough evidence to document its presence. Known as catamount by early settlers or *Lunk Soos* by the Wabanakis, it could terrorize the human inhabitants of a region as well as the deer and other prey, including moose. Adult males average about 160 pounds and can measure up to eight feet from nose to tip of tail. The mountain lion is perhaps one of the most efficient and effective hunters—muscular, wiry, armed with large claws and long canine teeth, and capable of forty-mile-an-hour running spurts. Today rumors of sightings persist, and it is possible that stragglers continue to hunt these woods along the waterway. If they do, then Smith Brook has much to offer.

At the head of the brook's cove the channel narrows and ledges begin to appear, jutting from the shore or rising out of the water—smooth, rounded, pinkish volcanic rock. The first of the outcrops is basalt, spewed out onto a seafloor between 450 and 475 million years ago during a major geologic disturbance known as the Taconic Orogeny. A short distance beyond, the exposed bedrock changes character, and for the next three miles the rock is of younger volcanics—about 400 million years old. It is here that the brook divides into

two slow-moving channels that encircle a mile-long ridge before reconnecting. Several fossil sites are near this junction. The glacially worn rock reveals fossils of simple aquatic animals such as corals, crinoids, and brachiopods.

This sluggish, meandering section of Smith Brook abounds with coves and terminates in a large pool nestled into low, converging hills. Upstream from the pool, the brook is youthful and swift moving. It shoots into the quiet pool through a narrow, straight sluiceway between ledges of volcanic rock. In late summer the yellowing grasses, pinkish outcrops, blues of the sky and water, and the greens of the forest vegetation create a secluded show of color.

A mountain lion as it might have stalked a white-tailed deer at Smith Brook near Eagle Lake. The presence of the mountain lion in Maine today is a subject of much speculation. Reports of sightings persist, including one in the Allagash in the fall of 1991.

Glacial deposits carried down to Eagle Lake by Russell Brook form a spectacular sand beach. Behind this 2,000-foot northern arm lies a vegetation-filled lagoon that attracts moose and deer.

Six miles up Eagle Lake, beneath the west-facing ledges of the Pump Handle, Russell Brook makes its entrance. Since glacial times the brook has been beach building, and most successfully. Particle by particle, a beach was created as the stream delivered a supply of sand from its streambed above. Shaped by wind, waves, and ice and held by plants, the deposits reflect a delicate balance among the forces of nature. Today a spectacular double-spit barrier beach closes the end of the cove.

A marshy lagoon behind the long stretch of sandy beach extends a perfect invitation to moose and other animals seeking a place to feed.

Two other brooks also add diversity to the shoreline. On the east side of the Pump Handle, Soper Brook enters the narrows of the lake, brushing the shore at the foot of the stand of old-growth pine. The small, winding cove, heavily wooded on both sides, leads to two small rapids, at the top of which is a pool beneath a falls. Even in late summer, swift, cold water tumbles over the fall's water-worn, four-foot-high ledge. Overhanging trees and the large purple-fringed orchis enhance the picturesque scene.

Soper Brook is one of several good trout habitats in the vicinity of Eagle Lake, according to Helen Hamlin, a warden's wife, schoolteacher, and writer whose book, *Nine Mile Bridge*, was published in 1945. She wrote, "From the fifteenth to the last day of May—before black-fly time—the only trout fishery in the country at that time is on Soper Brook."[18]

Up around the bend in a cove on the northern shore of the lake, Snare Brook makes an unobtrusive entrance. Following glacial outwash deposits of sand and gravel, the brook slows and begins a mile-long winding journey through a secluded deadwater marsh before reaching the lake. Moose, deer, and heron feed here undisturbed. Early morning can be full of surprises—one visitor reported seeing an adult black bear and two cubs walking along the shore. Evening also is a favorite feeding time, and a sunset over the large pines on the marsh's west bank can be unforgettable.

The Thoroughfare

At the northeastern corner of Eagle Lake the drainage flows north through a narrow channel. Beyond, it opens to another Round Pond, measuring about a mile in diameter, depending upon the water level. The terrain is low and flat, giving the impression of a high, elevated body of water. Though the pond is small, winds can sweep in quickly and churn the surface into high waves. At the pond's outlet end the forest closes in, and the passage into Churchill Lake stays relatively narrow for a mile and a half.

The Thoroughfare is a favorite place for moose. Their black hulks are easily seen along the low western shore of Round Pond and in the narrow waterway to Churchill Lake, cows and calves often feed along the shore. In summer the channel's deep, cold water attracts fish, which in turn invite loons and their young, ospreys, and bald eagles.

At the entrance to Churchill Lake, Thoroughfare Brook enters from the west. A forest of dead, gray trees pokes out of the marsh grasses, obscuring the main channel of the brook. Grassy banks further camouflage the main flow, and breaks in the evergreens surrounding this confusing cove are the only clues to the brook's course. In late summer the pied-billed grebe's (*Podilymbus podiceps*) mysterious laugh issues a challenge for a game of hide-and-seek.

Among the brook's multiple channels, moose feed in the privacy afforded by the high streambanks and tall marsh grasses. Beyond, the stream becomes more defined, and alders now provide a corridor of vegetation. The brook follows a glacially deposited finger of sand and gravel. A large American elm (*Ulmus americana*) confirms the swampy character of the surrounding land. Farther on the stream straightens; spruce and fir now shade the brook, and a large pool marks the beginning of shallow rapids. Here, eagles wait in a high tree, searching for fish. Four miles from Churchill Lake the brook branches like the tines of a fork and expands its watershed to ten square miles.

Moose calves feed on aquatic vegetation in the Thoroughfare. This channel connecting Eagle and Churchill lakes is a favorite spot for wildlife.

Churchill Lake and Heron Lake

On the shore of Churchill Lake at the foot of Churchill Ridge, the red fruit of northern mountain ash glow in the late afternoon sun. The lake's solitary island can be seen in the background.

Churchill Lake is the third-largest lake in the chain. Its appearance is deceiving, for at first glance it appears uninteresting—the shoreline seems fully revealed. Except for Churchill Ridge, which rises four hundred feet above the lake's surface on its north shore, and a small, rocky island that sits in the middle of the northern half of the lake, there appear to be no promising surprises—no discoveries to anticipate. But our northern lakes often are more than they might at first appear to be, as exploration soon reveals.

Churchill Lake is a little more than three miles long from its inlet to its outlet into Heron Lake, and its acreage is about one-third that of Chamberlain Lake's. Maximum depth is sixty-two feet, which helps to account for its abundance of burbot, brook and lake trout, and lake whitefish. There are many signs that fish are plentiful here; the presence of fishing mergansers, loons, osprey, and bald eagles suggest it and so does the ring-stippled surface following a mayfly hatch. A more direct observation is possible when the togue (lake trout) enter shallow waters to spawn in October.

After the ice leaves the lake in May, the pace of life quickens. The waves begin once more to rinse the beach with metronomic rhythm. The shore displays a burst of life as the hardwoods leaf out. Conifers distribute their pollen in copious clouds that, when backlighted, remind one of fresh snow blowing off the branches on a cold winter day.

On a mid-June day one might wake to the *oink-gawk-oink* of a flying raven (*Corvus corax*) announcing the morning's light. Out in the lake the caddis-fly and mayfly hatch is on, and on land the black flies, mosquitos, and midges are in season. Butterflies gather on bare, moist soil near the water. Deer feed on tender shoots of grass in openings along the shore. In the distance the *wha, wha, wha* of a snipe interrupts the quiet. Somewhere a moose grunts an apparent response. From across the lake the alarm cry of a loon suggests a perceived threat. On the south shore a pair of eagles watch from a tall dead pine.

As the day wears on, the deep wavering buzz of hummingbirds, drawing nectar from the spring flowers, vibrates the air. The warming sun enhances the smell of pine needles. Afternoon brings the distant rumble of thunder, and attention shifts skyward to the ragged, gray, drooping veil of an approaching shower. It passes to the east. The late afternoon hoot of a barred owl brings Churchill Ridge to life, dispelling the myth that darkness is the only time this night hunter gives its call. Dusk comes late in June, and life continues its wanderings. The last light of day records the vague, silent silhouette of a moose swimming across the narrows between Heron and Churchill lakes.

PLEASANT STREAM

To anyone who loves the sights and sounds of wilderness, Pleasant Stream is aptly named. In June, deer are likely to be feeding near the marshy edge of the stream's mouth, always ready to jump to the safety of the dense growth along the shore. Bullfrogs, hidden among the marshy weeds and dry-ki, send their calls from one side of the broad, shallow inlet cove to the other. Where the cove turns to the left, beavers make evening forays from a low, flat house on the muddy bank. The channel narrows, and riffles increase as the current quickens.

Above the small stretch of fast water, the soft, blue-green needles of tamarack close upon the stream as it flows quietly through a small bog-forest ecosystem. Along with the tamarack, black spruce is another distinctive tree for this kind of wetland, and occasionally northern white cedar invades where nutrients are more plentiful and the water less acid. But at this place on Pleasant Stream, it is tamarack that dominates the pioneering bog-forest. The tree's widely spaced, needle-tufted branches let light shine through, allowing shrubs to grow beneath it, including alders, blueberries, and cranberries. The tamarack grows on a grounded mat of mosses and heath plants, and, like the black spruce, has the ability to produce new sets of roots from its trunk or branches as the mat deepens. The tamarack's shallow root system may spread wider than its height, thus giving some protection against wind-throw. Another danger it faces is defoliation by the larch sawfly (*Pristiphora erichsonii*).

In May and June the spring warblers arrive just as the first insect larvae are beginning to devour the newly opened leaves. They include the Nashville, magnolia, blackburnian, bay-breasted, black-throated green, Canada (*Wilsonia canadensis*), Cape May, and yellow (*Dendroica petechia*) warblers. Many of these migrants, such as the Nashville warbler, may stay and breed here. The large tracts of forest in the north woods are ideal for these birds, which tend to build open, cup-shaped nests in trees or on the ground. In suburban areas where woodlands are fragmented, these birds are more vulnerable to predation.

Other life thrives along the stream. The pumping sound of the American bittern signals the beginning of its mating urges. Mergansers also take advantage of the stream's remoteness to raise their families. In the upper reaches beaver have built a series of dams and a large house in one of the ponds. An old cedar at the edge of the stream still sports evidence of an unsuccessful, long-ago attempt by the beaver to fell it.

A visit in early October finds Pleasant Stream at low water. The cow moose are now under the watchful eyes of bulls. Migrating birds are visitors to the stream. Small flocks of Canada geese (*Branta canadensis*) find brief refuge, and pairs of greater yellowlegs (*Tringa melanoleuca*), distinguished from the lesser yellowlegs (*Tringa flavipes*) by their knobby knees, search the shallow waters in the cove for food. Along the shore the grasses, sedges, and rushes are rapidly losing their green and changing to dull golden brown. The tamarack are beginning to turn yellow as they enter the first stage of losing their needles, and the many hardwoods along the edge are now at peak color.

TWIN BROOKS

Two additional tributaries flow into the southeast corner of Churchill Lake—North Twin Brook and South Twin Brook. The north brook drains Spider Lake, a distance of about two miles from Churchill Lake. The current is always swift in this small stream, even in late July in a normal season. The mouth of the brook's divided channels are obscured by dry-ki. Here, on a low grassy mound among stumps and logs, loons sometimes elect to build a nest. At the first sign of danger, a nesting loon flattens itself head-down, facing the water, so that at any moment it can easily slide in. Upstream the channels merge, and the brook flows out of the forest from beneath overhanging speckled alders, providing a protected place for deer to feed.

South Twin Brook is located a half mile down the shore from its northern twin. Together, the two brooks have delivered material to create a shallow, sandy-bottomed cove. Beneath the water, wave action has fretted the sandy bottom with a beautiful pattern of ripples. South Twin Brook is a little over a mile in length, flowing out of Twin Lake and Cliff Lake. Smaller than its northern twin, it, too, emerges from beneath a crowded canopy of alders.

CHURCHILL RIDGE

Churchill Ridge, on the north shore of the lake, wears well—not only because it provides a beautiful and interesting backdrop for the lake but also because it is made of tough, 450-million-year-old volcanic rock. In true glaciated fashion, its south-facing side drops steeply to the lake.

The slopes of the ridge are covered by a northern hardwood forest mixed with conifers. Sugar maple, American beech, eastern hemlock, yellow birch, white pine, paper birch, and trembling aspen are present, among others. Conifers favor the top of the ridge, and striped maple (*Acer pensylvanicum*) is present in the understory on the slopes. On the forest floor of the open woods, a variety of herbaceous plants grow, as William O. Douglas discovered on his trip through the region around 1960.[19] Among the plants he observed poking up from the rich humus were oxalis (*Oxalis* sp.), wild iris (*Iris* sp.), trillium (*Trillium* sp.), violet (*Viola* sp.), pinedrop (probably *Pterosporo andromedea*), common self-heal, silverweed cinquefoil (probably *Potentilla argentea*), hooked buttercup (*Ranunculus recurvatus*), marsh St.-John's-wort (*Hypericum virginicum*), butter-and-eggs toadflax (*Linaria vulgaris*), meadowsweet, goldthread (*Coptis groenlandica*), and the ground ivy run-away-robin (*Glechoma hederacea*).

In spring, the southerly exposed slope responds earliest to the more direct, longer-lasting rays of the sun. As the snow begins to melt, first in the open hardwoods, summer birds start arriving from their southern wintering areas.

Among them is the ruby-throated hummingbird (*Archilochus colubris*), which sometimes arrives weeks before the spring flowers bloom. How does it survive without nectar? It is known to feed on sap collected in holes drilled in trees by the yellow-bellied sapsucker (*Sphyrapicus varius*), which arrives about a month before the hummingbird. The sap has chemical similarities to nectar.

By mid-June life on the ridge is in full progress. The deciduous canopy is now closed. Sunflecks sweep the forest floor, dappling the leaves with enough light for the photosynthesis required to meet the minimum survival needs of the herbaceous plants. Canada mayflower is already in full bloom; this perennial's shoots were produced the previous fall and overwintered near the soil's surface. Bunchberry is beginning to bloom, with some of its blossoms still turning from green to white. Wild sarsaparilla's (*Aralia nudicaulis*) ball-like, fuzzy clusters of flowers stand sheltered beneath the plant's large umbrella of leaflets.

Insects are also present in large numbers in June. And so are the birds. The white-throated sparrow (*Zonotrichia albicollis*), dark-eyed junco (*Junco hyemalis*), Canada warbler, mourning warbler (*Oporornis philadelphia*), and hermit thrush (*Catharus guttatus*) are building nests and laying eggs among the ground plants. A few feet above the ground, at the shrub level, the black-throated blue warbler (*Dendroica caerulescens*), American redstart (*Setophaga ruticilla*), solitary vireo (*Vireo solitarius*), and black-capped chickadee have their nesting under way. In the upper story, cedar waxwings (*Bombycilla cedrorum*) are looking for nesting sites in the open hardwoods, while the purple finch is seeking out a conifer location. Yellow-bellied sapsuckers are nesting in holes.

On the forest floor, by the middle of June, snowshoe hares are already about to bear their second litter. Many of the young red squirrels still remain in their nests in tree cav-

A male ruby-throated hummingbird, arriving in the north woods before nectar-producing wildflowers are in bloom, finds a nutritious substitute in holes drilled in an eastern hemlock by a yellow-bellied sapsucker.

ities. Young porcupines (*Erethizon dorsatum*), some perhaps only in their second week, are feeding on the ground-level plants. In dense thickets the white-tailed deer are bearing their fawns.

The spring and summer seasons are short; the first frost could come as early as August, and by late summer, signs of the seasonal change are appearing. On the forest floor great numbers of fungi, hidden until now, poke up from beneath the soil and leaf litter to reveal their mushroom reproductive fruiting structures. Nuts are developing on the beeches, and squirrels are beginning to cache their winter supplies. The most visible change, however, is yet to come.

September and October bring about spectacular color changes in the leaves of the deciduous trees before they drop to the ground. Cool nights and shortened days trigger the cells between the leaves and stems to cut off water and minerals. The green chlorophyll, once so abundant that it masked the other pigments in the leaves, breaks down and reveals the reds, yellows, and other color pigments that have been there all along. Churchill Ridge turns into a pageant of unforgettable beauty.

Helen Hamlin, who lived within sight of the ridge for several years in the early 1940s, wrote about this fall performance:

> October in the north woods is breathtakingly beautiful. The days are warm, lazy and calm. The lakes are mirrors reflecting the deep blue of the skies and gaudily colored, panoramic shores—golden beeches, crimson maples, bright-yellow birches, wine-colored ash, and background of dark spruces and firs and lavender distances. The season is short—as short as a north woods spring—and Nature indulges in all her capricious fancies to make it a brilliant one.[20]

Thirty years later, Dorothy Kidney at Lock Dam gave month-by-month impressions of the changes around these lakes as fall and winter approached.[21] August: "The mosquitoes, blackflies and minges are about gone. Days are mellow and nights are cooler. Fireflies still wink and twinkle at the edge of the stream. . . . Canada jays are our constant companions lately, . . . bold, fearless and always hungry." September: "Days are clear and often warm. . . . The lakes are frequently calm and the days are mellow and golden with a crispness after the sun goes down." October: "Frost in the night and the temperature dropped to nineteen degrees Fahrenheit above zero. Flocks of wild geese heading South flew over." November: "The sky turns gray and frost is on the grass early in the morning. . . . Rabbits' fur is turning white. And thin ice is making in the coves now, waiting to lock all these lakes from shore to shore in its deep, frigid grip."

HERON LAKE

The low water of late summer and fall frequently leaves only a small connecting channel between Churchill Lake and Heron Lake at the end of Churchill Ridge. A spit of sandy beach trails off into the smaller lake in response to the increasing current near the head of the river. Eroded lines and undercuts along the edge of the beach also record the lowering water levels. The lake is small, more like a pond. The tall, whitened stumps of dead trees stand scattered along the channel near the steeper east shore. The opposite shore is marshy and shallower—a favorite of deer and moose. The lake narrows, and the sound of rapids grows louder.

In early fall, northern hardwoods on Churchill Ridge
create a spectacular backdrop for Churchill Lake.

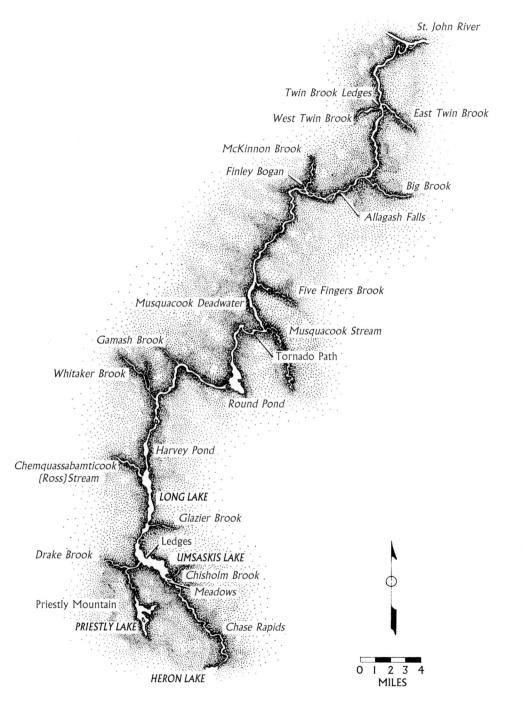

The River

St. John River

Twin Brook Ledges

West Twin Brook

East Twin Brook

McKinnon Brook

Finley Bogan

Big Brook

Allagash Falls

Five Fingers Brook

Musquacook Deadwater

Musquacook Stream

Gamash Brook

Tornado Path

Whitaker Brook

Round Pond

Harvey Pond

Chemquassabamticook
(Ross) Stream

LONG LAKE

Glazier Brook

Ledges

Drake Brook

UMSASKIS LAKE

Chisholm Brook

Meadows

Priestly Mountain

PRIESTLY LAKE

Chase Rapids

HERON LAKE

0 1 2 3 4
MILES

Perhaps it was ground out by the glacier or perhaps it was the result of an ancient fold or a weakness in the bedrock, but for whatever reason the site where the Allagash lakes spill over their basins and rush northward occurs at the end of Heron Lake. It would seem altogether natural with so much pent-up energy stored in the large lakes above that the release be wild and turbulent, and this expectation is amply fulfilled by the whitewater below Heron Lake.

The Allagash River winds through hilly country for sixty-two miles, dropping more than three hundred feet before meeting the St. John. Except for a few rest stops in small lakes, ponds, and deadwaters, the river's current remains energetic throughout its length, exposing dark gray slates and cutting through mounds of earth that parallel the last glacial flow. In its more gentle stretches, the river mirrors hillsides of northern hardwood, lowlands of conifers, and floodplains of silver maples (*Acer saccharinum*) and willows. As it moves northward, it leaves behind the red spruce and enters the domain of the white and black spruces.

The Allagash is a magnet for animal life. Throughout its length a remarkable diversity of animals are attracted to its innumerable habitats. The alternating rapids and pools, the boulder-strewn bottoms and sandy beds, and the tributary brooks and streams meet the needs of such animals as brook trout, wood turtles, moose, deer, otter, mink, and beaver. The beaver are distinguished by their ability to engineer streams to meet their own needs, and in so doing they benefit many of the river's other inhabitants.

The river exhibits its own unique pattern of change, and life adapts to its idiosyncrasies. During warm summer days when the river is lower and quieter, the wood turtle is enticed to laze on logs along the water's edge. In winter the wood turtle retires to the mud, and the river runs quietly beneath a cover of ice and snow. Later, as the climate warms and the wood turtle begins to stir, the river rises in meeting the challenge presented by the spring snowmelt. In summer its personality once again alters as it displays a more gentle, immediate response to the rains and runoff with which it must contend. Thus, throughout the year the mood and manner of the river changes, reflecting the unique character of this north woods country.

The Allagash River begins as a large pool after leaving Heron Lake through Churchill Dam, giving no hint of the wild, turbulent character it will take on in Chase Rapids below.

THE RAPIDS

The most turbulent stretch of the river, Chase Rapids, runs from Heron Lake to Umsaskis Lake, a distance of approximately nine miles. A thick forest of spruce and fir mixed with northern white cedar, poplar, white birch, and other hardwood species lines the riverbanks. Dead trees along the edge are clothed with beard lichen. The river here is narrow, averaging seventy-five feet in width, with many twists and turns. The riverbed is strewn with boulders, and the water swirls wildly over and around them. It drops quickly, nine feet per mile on an average, and the steepest drops, with whitewater and standing waves, occur within the first three miles. A mile below the lake, the water boils over a two-foot drop.

It was near these rapids in December 1901 that hunters reported seeing a herd of seven caribou.[1] This was the last authenticated sighting of Maine's caribou herd. Today moose and deer are the only hoofed mammals seen along this stretch of the river, but encounters with them can be no less memorable. This writer witnessed one rarely seen event here in early March of 1992 involving a deer and a coyote.[2] It was a scene of tense drama. For almost an hour the stark reality of survival for the creatures in these north woods was unexpectedly revealed.

The river that day was low and clear of ice. Deep snow, reflecting brilliantly white in the late afternoon sun, separated the forest from the river on its east shore and capped the boulders strewn across the rapids at the third drop. Two deer, tails up and eyes wide, suddenly appeared on the west side and bounded up the shore, their jumps rendered soundless by the roar of the rapids and the deep snow. One disappeared back into the woods, but the other, without hesitation, plunged into the icy water.

As the deer neared the opposite shore, a coyote was running among the trees beyond. The deer, evidently sensing danger, stopped in the river and hunkered down in the water behind a large boulder near the shore. The coyote appeared on the bank downstream and then, spotting the deer, flattened itself in the snow. For ten to fifteen minutes the deer remained in its place. The coyote never moved. Tentatively the deer began to wade toward shore; the coyote tensed, raised up, and leaned forward. Leaving the water, the deer climbed the bank and shook itself dry.

The coyote began to stalk the deer, increasing its speed with every step. Seeing it coming, the deer leaped back into the river, heading for the shore from which it had come. The coyote hesitated for a moment at the water's edge, and then it, too, leaped into the rapids behind the frantic deer. As its quarry approached the shore, the coyote climbed a rock in the middle of the rapids. At that point it saw the human observers and aborted the chase, making a wet and hasty retreat back to the safety of the woods. The deer again stopped in the water, as if unsure of its next move; then it, too, bounded on into the woods. Once again the river became the focus—beautiful in the late afternoon, betraying none of the tense action that had occurred only moments before.

Although wild animals are drawn to the Allagash throughout its length, some creatures especially favor its rapids. Flowing over a rough bed of pebble-to boulder-sized rocks, alternatingly deep and quiet, then shallow and quick, Chase Rapids provides ideal conditions for brook trout. The turbulent waters are well aerated here, and oxygen is abundant. Riffles and pools provide many protected nooks and crannies and promote the growth of algae and other organic matter that support the food web of insects, small fish, and other organisms upon which the trout depend.

Near Umsaskis Lake the rapids widen to well over one hundred feet, and pools become larger and deeper. Aquatic plants gain an easier foothold, and they, in turn, attract moose. Two miles before the lake, the river flattens and meanders around gravel bars and grassy islands. The rattle and splash of the rapids is replaced by quiet once again, but those who have seen the rapids do not forget them. For Henry Baldwin, who traversed the length of the river in 1963, "these rapids remain in memory as the most beautiful stretch of the river."[3]

A large male coyote pursues a white-tailed deer on the bank of Chase Rapids at the head of the Allagash River. The coyote has replaced the timber wolf as the largest wild canine in this region.

UMSASKIS LAKE

Remote Umsaskis Lake is beautifully situated in hilly country. Its diverse shoreline exhibits varied topography and a mixture of trees and shrubs that provide a variety of habitats for wildlife. One of the richest wildlife areas is encountered at the lake's inlet end.

THE MEADOWS

The rapids at the head of the Allagash River flow directly into a large marsh called Umsaskis Meadows. Several brooks also feed into the marsh, among them Chisholm Brook, which enters on the east shore. This and the other small streams here are well watered because of the extensive drainage area between Umsaskis and the Musquacook lakes to the east. Chisholm Brook is small and rocky, and in summer, grasses and sedges crowd near its mouth, along with a large population of water striders. The smaller enchanter's nightshade (*Circaea quadrisulcata*) is found in the cool, moist environment of the brook. The plant's unusual white flowers have paired parts—two sepals, two petals, and two stamens. The moist soil conditions also favor turtlehead (*Chelone glabra*), a member of the figwort family, whose creamy white petals, arranged in an egg shape, give the flower its name.

Since glacial times the river and brooks have deposited their loads of sediments at Umsaskis meadows, building the marsh at an almost imperceptible rate. Now the river winds its way through the wetland for about a mile and a half before emerging into the open water of Umsaskis Lake. The slow-moving, oxygenated waters create a productive environment by supplying minerals and contributing to rapid decay and the recycling of nutrients.

In summer the wetland is covered with rushes, sedges, and grasses, including wild rice (*Zizania aquatica*). A maze of shallow, muddy, weedy channels, many concealed by dense stands of speckled alder, weave through the half-mile width of wetland. The bright yellows of swamp

With its neck outstretched and bill pointed upward to imitate marsh grasses, an American bittern adopts a hiding posture in Umsaskis Meadows.

A downy woodpecker, one of several species of
woodpeckers that live in the waterway, alights on
a dead tree to begin a search for insects.

candles, dark purple-reds of swamp milkweed, pinks of meadowsweet, whites of tall meadow rue, and purples of the large purple fringed orchis all color the channel banks. Periscopic eyes of green frogs peer up from grassy pools. Old beaver dams, now well vegetated, continue to enclose small ponds among the alders. But what most brings the marsh to life are its birds.

Abundant water, varied shelters, and diversity of food organisms make the marsh a haven for birdlife. The spring and summer seasons, especially, are busy times for establishing and protecting territories, courting, nesting, and rearing. The sights and sounds are captivating: the eerie flight-sound of the common snipe in its territorial dives; the pumping *gunk-gha, gunk-gha* of the American bittern; the alarmed squawk of the great blue heron, with its slow, rhythmic flight and easy glide; the rattling call of the belted kingfisher and its ospreylike pre-dive hover; the rusty, unoiled cry of the red-winged blackbird (*Agelaius phoeniceus*); and the *zzzt* of the high-flying common nighthawk (*Chordeiles minor*).

Trees in the marsh furnish nesting places for many of the birds. Cavities provide homes for the wood duck (*Aix sponsa*), hooded merganser (*Lophodytes cucullatus*), common merganser, barred owl, tree swallow, downy woodpecker (*Picoides pubescens*), and pileated woodpecker. Such birds as the yellow warbler and eastern kingbird build in the branches of trees. In low vegetation, just above the marsh's water level, the red-winged blackbird, swamp sparrow, American bittern, and pied-billed grebe construct their nests. Where the ground is dry on rises near the edge of the marsh, the black duck, blue-winged teal (*Anas discors*), killdeer (*Charadrius vociferus*), spotted sandpiper, common snipe, savannah sparrow (*Passerculus sandwichensis*), yellow-throated warbler (*Dendroica dominica*), and red-breasted mer-

A lone meadowsweet plant finds a foothold on the rocky shore beneath the ledges of Umsaskis Lake.

ganser (*Mergus serrator*) nest. By midsummer most of the nestlings have fledged, and the young waterfowl venture out along the shore of the lake under the protective watch of their parents.

THE LAKE

Umsaskis lake is about three miles long and more than a half mile wide. Its orientation suggests strong glacial influence. The maximum depth of fifty-eight feet provides the cold-water habitat preferred by brook trout and lake trout. The varied topography of the thickly forested shoreline ranges from steep slopes and precipitous ledges to flat floodplains, marshes, and swamps.

Hidden beneath the summer's quilt of vegetation, the land is blanketed with glacial till—an unsorted mixture of sand, silt, clay, and stones deposited directly on the bedrock of slate and metamorphosed sandstone. This glacial evidence is not unusual for this region except in one regard: glacial scratches on the outcrops show movement of the ice sheet toward the northwest and north, almost opposite in direction to the other flows. Geologists now believe that these striations represent the glacier's later flows. They theorize that they occurred as a result of a large ice dome in the region. Being higher in elevation than the valley of the St. Lawrence River to the north, the ice flowed briefly in that direction.

It took thousands of years, following the disappearance of the glacier, to produce the dark gray silts and sandy loams that characterize the topsoils here. The soils favor a northern hardwood forest mixed with the conifers and an understory that includes woodferns, partridgeberry (*Mitchella repens*), checkerberry (*Gaultheria procumbens*), and starflower.

Winter dramatically transforms the lake and its surrounding forest. Annette Jackson, who lived on Umsaskis Lake for seven years in the 1930s with her husband, a gamewarden, left a vivid impression of this landscape in her book *My Life in the Maine Woods:*

> The hush of the woods in winter is often so heavy that you begin to think of it as something more than silence. At times it is like a strong kind of mist beyond the power of your eyes to see, yet so real you want to reach out and push it aside and let some sound come in. The quieter it is, the harder you strain your ears, without knowing why you are listening. But when the hush is suddenly broken by a sound, you realize that in the still clear air the range of your hearing has increased. You hear the bark of a fox out in the hills, or the hoot of an owl, and often enough . . . I have heard a mouse snore. When the ice has formed and is four or five feet thick on the lake, it begins to crack. You know about it because the noise it makes in the night is like many shotguns going off at one time. Sometimes you hear a grating sound like a monster grinding its teeth. The lake is only stretching in its sleep.[4]

BEAVER

Spring is when the young of most animals that live in the Allagash are born. Births are early enough in the season to ensure that offspring achieve a measure of independence and maturity before the rigors of winter set in. The beaver is a good example. Found throughout North America, this large, semi-aquatic rodent is especially adapted to the north woods, and the streams and lakes of the waterway provide many ideal locations for it to live. One such place is Drake Brook, not far from where Annette Jackson lived. It flows into Umsaskis Lake on the the west side, where it has deposited a large delta of deep, silty soil. Alders, grasses, sedges, ferns, and other herbaceous plants grow in profusion on the wet land and become part of the beaver's spring diet.

The narrow stream, flowing between muddy banks and alders, provides a ready opportunity for dam building and the construction of a house in the deepest water. Beaver homes have at least two underwater entrances. The inside chamber of a house has a floor bedded with shredded wood, dry mosses, and grasses. The house is protected by two-to-three-foot-thick walls at the bottom. The top is thinner and looser, with openings for ventilation.

In mid-May to early June an average of three to five kits are born, each weighing a pound or less. By November they will weigh nearly sixteen pounds. The young stay with the family for about two years and then move out in the spring to found their own colonies.

Spring is an active time in a beaver colony. Dam and house building and repair are undertaken. Canals are dug to food trees such as aspens and willows. During these activities, adult beaver murmur and "talk" incessantly. An occasional sharp slap of a tail on the water signals danger.

The ponds also attract a host of other wildlife species, including wood ducks and other waterfowl, muskrats, moose, deer, and many predators—mink, foxes, bobcats (*Lynx rufus*), and coyotes.

PRIESTLY LAKE

A major tributary of Drake Brook flows out of Priestly Lake. This remote body of water, about two miles south and slightly west of Umsaskis Lake, is deep, irregularly shaped, and surrounded by steep hills and mountains. A forest of spruce, fir, and cedar descends to its edge. The narrow shore affords cover for mink and other animals that hunt around water. A few large dead white pines stand above the lake's margin, providing vantage points for raptors and kingfishers. Several islands break

up the lake, adding to its uneven outline. Occasionally moose emerge from the dense woods, especially at the shallower south end, where conditions are more conducive to wading.

The trail from Umsaskis Lake to Priestly passes through a low swamp densely populated with spruce and fir. Sphagnum mosses carpet much of the forest floor, and there is much cover for wildlife. A reported sighting of a black bear here serves as a reminder that this large north woods mammal is present, although it is usually shy and avoids contact with humans. Farther along, the trail passes through scattered hemlock and openings where raspberries and fireweed abound. In shaded areas ferns form a dense ground cover; lady fern (*Athyrium filix-femina*), ostrich fern (*Matteuccia struthiopteris*), and bracken fern (*Pteridium aquilinum*) are all present. Running ground pine (*Lycopodium complanatum*), a fern relative, is also prevalent. In heavily wooded swamps near the lake, Labrador tea, shining club moss (*Lycopodium lucidulum*), clintonia (*Clintonia borealis*), sheep laurel, and a variety of sphagnum mosses grow. Among the low plants are tracks of coyote, deer, and moose.

After following the west shore of the lake for a relatively short distance, the trail ascends the steep north slope of Priestly Mountain. A short distance below the mountain's top grows an old forest of undisturbed northern hardwoods. Yellow birch, sugar maple, and American beech dominate this hillside stand. All three species are shade tolerant, and beneath them grow many of their progeny. Dense carpets of wood sorrel and club moss cover the ground around their roots. In early August the red fruit of twisted-stalk (*Streptopus amplexifolius*) adds a touch of color to the understory.

The thin forest soils of Priestly Mountain cover the largest body of igneous rock in the river section of the waterway. Known as the Priestly granodiorite, the rock is the commonest member of the granite family. Its coarse grain and min-

A large beaver dam extends across the mouth of
Drake Brook at Umsaskis Lake. Newly cut speckled alders
indicate that the dam is being actively maintained.

eral makeup of light-colored quartz and feldspar with flecks of dark biotite mica and hornblende is characteristic of intrusive rocks that formed from the cooling of magma deep below the earth's surface. The rock is old, formed in Devonian times, somewhere around 400 million years ago.

So distinctive is this rock in an area where slate and other metamorphosed sedimentary rocks predominate that its removal and transport by the last glacier give evidence of the direction and duration of the glacier's flows. Erratic boulders of the granodiorite rest on the landscape surrounding the mountain and show a strong pattern of dispersal southeast of the mountain and some scattering to the northwest. This pattern supports the evidence that the glacier flowed here in different directions at different times.

Priestly Mountain affords good views of Umsaskis and Long lakes. The ledges on the far shore of Umsaskis Lake can be seen from this vantage point, as well as the delta of Drake Brook on the near shore.

THE LEDGES

The Priestly granodiorite pluton extends under Umsaskis Lake, and in one place, at least, it grades into quartz monzonite, another pluton-affiliated rock. On the east shore of Umsaskis Lake, opposite Drake Brook, the monzonite contacts an outstanding ledge bluff of weathered, metamorphosed sandstone shot through with resistant quartz veins. Due to differential weathering, the veins stand out in relief from the softer sandstone, appearing to enclose some of the rocks in a net. The effect of long exposure to the elements is also made evident by the sharp, angled pieces of rock that have broken away and now lie along the shore beneath the outcrop.

The shore is home for swamp candles, blue vetch (*Vica cracca*), swamp milkweed, and species of goldenrod. Higher on the ledges, all stages of succession are exhibited. Foliose and crustose lichens are well established, and star moss (*Mnium cuspidatum*), grasses, and raspberry have gained a foothold. Common, or golden, polypody fern (*Polypodium virginianum*) grows out of crevices, as does pale corydalis. Other herbaceous plants include sheep sorrel and mouse-ear hawkweed (*Hieracium pilosella*). Meadowsweet and balsam poplar (*Populus balsamifera*), balsam fir, white pine, trembling aspen, and northern white cedar also populate the ledge.

The top of the bluff gives a fine view of the lake, which is especially beautiful in the evening when the setting sun highlights the shades of green on the opposite shore. A narrow, light green band of alders fronts the darker evergreens and deciduous trees. Priestly Mountain, in the distance, caps the monocolored array with more dark evergreens. Unless one knows about the pluton of igneous rock from which the mountain is made, there is little to connect that distant peak with this ledge bluff on the shore of Umsaskis Lake.

Priestly Lake, surrounded by privately owned land, is a remote body of water connected to Umsaskis Lake by Drake Brook. Beyond the far shore, Priestly Mountain overlooks the lake. The mountain is formed of granitic igneous rock, unusual in this region, where slate and other metamorphosed sedimentary rocks predominate.

Pale corydalis, a member of the poppy family, is
found in crevices of dry, rocky outcrops along
the shores and islands in the waterway.

Long Lake

As seen from the top of Priestly Mountain, Umsaskis Lake narrows between low hills at its north end until only a small thoroughfare channels its waters into Long Lake, a long ribbon of water stretching northward. Entering the shallow narrows to Long Lake, the river tugs briefly once again. Within a short distance, the lake becomes a deep forty-eight feet, meeting the stringent temperature and oxygen requirements of the brook and lake trout.

To the right of the entrance to Long Lake, Glazier Brook is building a marshy delta; with help from the river currents, it now spreads more than a half mile down the shore. The shoreline beyond is backed by low, undulating hills—knolls and ridges of glacial till left by the melting of stagnated glacial ice. The moraine that formed under these conditions continues down the east shore of the lake, then influences the path of the river's channel for the next ten miles to yet another Round Pond.

On an early midsummer morning, when the first rays of the sun creep over the hills, the west shore of the lake becomes vibrant with color and activity. Close to the lake's edge the shoreline reveals details unseen from the middle of the lake. It is an in-and-out shore of projecting sandbars and points enclosing the marshy outlets of small brooks and seeps. Strips of speckled alder border the shore, and at the water's edge the dew-laden red leaves of sundew put on a dazzling display in the early sunlight. In open areas the fernlike leaves of yarrow (*Achillea millefolium*) mingle with grasses, and in sandy places the yellow blossoms of common evening primrose (*Oenothera biennis*) brighten the shore. The waters are shallow, and emergent plants abound—cattails, reeds, sedges, rushes. In deeper water the floating-leaved plants cover the surface: water lilies—including yellow-pond, or bullhead, lily—pondweed (*Potamogeton* sp.), and smartweed (*Polygonum* sp.). Dragonflies and damselflies dart and hover, resting briefly on the aquatic plants.

Every corner brings new surprises—goldeneye ducks (*Bucephala clangula*), great blue herons, American bitterns, merganser ducks, and red-winged blackbirds. Flycatchers watch from the alders. Belted kingfishers on overhanging branches intently scan the waters. Ospreys occasionally rest on higher treetops. Deer, reddish in the sunshine, stand in the shallow water, feeding on grasses and water plants.

As morning wears on and the sun rises higher, breezes increase and the murmur of waves on the shore provides a soothing background. Close to the wooded shore, a recurrent snapping *plop* tells of spruce cones hitting the forest floor—the harvesting activities of red squirrels are in full progress.

CHEMQUASSABAMTICOOK STREAM

Several miles down the west shore, a beautiful sand beach intrudes into the lake. Its profile highlights the picturesque view of the lake's shore. When low fog rolls in and the waters are quiet, the beach appears to hover in space. Beyond, a large, low, flat delta creeps out into the lake, choking off all but a narrow channel. The source of this mass of silt and sand is Chemquassabamticook Stream, now also called Ross Stream. It is a major tributary of the river, rising out of a large lake by the same name thirteen crow-flight miles to the southwest (based on the shaky assumption that a crow flies in a straight line)—roughly twenty-three miles by stream.

At its mouth the stream cuts down through the deep silt to enter Long Lake at the southern edge of its delta. Here its load of silts and sands is borne by the lake's current into Harvey Pond at the end of Long Lake. With every spring's flooding, new sediment is spread over the delta and into the lake.

In summer the stream meanders between high banks of deposited sediment. Newly cut embankments reveal distinct layers, a record of past floods. Dead-end backwaters, set deep in the delta, hide feeding deer, moose, and waterfowl. The streambed itself is gravelly and pebbly. Inside curves are marked by gravel-cobble bars, while outside corners are high, stream-cut, silty banks that support dense stands of purple-red swamp milkweed, water parsnip, yellow swamp candles, blue vetch, pink-blossomed thistle (*Circium* sp.), bright green sensitive ferns, and tall plumed grasses. The banks are pocked with the holes of nesting bank swallows (*Riparia riparia*) and

some that might even harbor the nests of belted kingfishers. Beavers are active here, too, as some tributaries are held back by small dams.

Upstream beyond the delta, the current quickens and riffles and pools increase. Occasional elm trees grow on the banks. A large meadow extends for about three miles upstream on the south side. Tamaracks grow in lower portions of the meadow and other conifers are interspersed throughout. Above the meadow the stream continues, becoming increasingly narrow and shallow. Four miles west of Long Lake, the tributary leading to Cunliff Lake enters. From here the stream wends its way through hilly country to Clayton Lake, then on to Chemquassabamticook Lake.

Early morning fog shrouds Long Lake near the mouth of Chemquassabamticook Stream.

The River to Round Pond

Long Lake becomes a river again two miles beyond Chemquassabamticook Stream. It passes into a large pool, overflows a shallow gravelly basin, and runs down a set of riffles. Thus the pattern is established—pools alternating with riffles or rapids. This is repeated throughout the river's journey to the St. John. Some of the pools appear as long deadwaters, but inevitably the roiling sounds of rapids signal the end of quiet water.

The banks are lined with spruce and fir interspersed with northern white cedar and white birch. Shaggy, dead branches of trees support the familiar soft, yellow-gray-green strands of beard lichen. Many dead trees overhang the river or lie along its edge. Where small streams and brooks enter, small pocket meadows of grasses and alders appear.

Whittaker Brook is one of the many small streams emerging from the forest. It comes in on the west shore two and one half miles below Harvey Pond. Here William O. Douglas explored and found the shore colored with the tiny, deep golden yellow flowers of St.-John's-wort (*Hypericum* sp.), the yellow creeping spearwort buttercup (*Ranunculus reptans*), upright yellow wood-sorrel (*Oxalis stricta*), blue-flowered and white-eyed brook lobelia (*Lobelia kalmii*), red clover (*Trifolium pratense*), wild strawberry (*Fragaria virginiana*), common pearly everlasting (*Anaphalis margaritacea*), red-orange hawkweed (*Hieracium aurantiacum*), and ox-eye daisy (*Chrysanthemum leucanthemum*).[5] He left the river and followed Whittaker Brook, where he encountered bush cinquefoil blooming yellow, meadow rue, velvetleaf blueberry (*Vaccinium myrtilloides*), and a member of the mustard family—whitish flowered wild radish, also called jointed charlock (*Raphanus raphanistrum*).

The river alternately widens and narrows, flowing fast then slow on its way to Round Pond. Sunlight, let in between the trees, lights the river's cobbly-gravelly bottom and the waving, downstream-pointing fronds of grasses and other aquatic vegetation. The river's channel, the deepest part of its bed, meanders from bank to bank. Grassy islands, some with trees, and long gravel bars also divert the flow. Kingfishers follow the river, staking out their private fishing areas. Mergansers and goldeneyes follow it, too. Great blue herons fish the edges and backwaters, sometimes resting in trees or on rocks and logs at the river's edge.

At Gamash Brook the river makes an acute swing to the southeast and heads for the pond below. Soon it broadens. Gravelly bars and islands become more numerous, forming large, low, grassy hummocks, and the river braids, dividing into three channels. Willows, elms, and dead trees line the banks, standing well above the profuse "hedges" of speckled alder. Large clumps of swamp milkweed grow on the grassy banks. Near the pond, the south channel's steep right side is populated with spruce and fir; alders mediate between them and the water.

The shallow channels and the lush vegetation surrounding them are ideal habitat for birds. A large dead elm is often decorated with roosting swallows—as many as seventy-five at one time have been counted. Canada geese take up residence here, along with pied-billed grebes, American bitterns, great blue herons, goldeneye ducks, and black ducks. Chickadees, white-breasted nuthatches (*Sitta carolinensis*), kingbirds, and yellow warblers flutter about the edges of the channels. And beyond is the pond.

Below Long Lake, the Allagash River flows
between banks lined with spruce and fir.

Round Pond

This Round Pond is more oblong than it is round, being about three-quarters of a mile wide and two miles long. It nestles in hills as high as fifteen hundred feet forested with conifers and many species of northern hardwoods. The pond is 130 feet below the level of Churchill Lake where the river began. Its deepest hole is thirty-six feet below its surface—deep enough for a healthy brook trout population, which shares the pond with lake whitefish and round whitefish. The pond's surrounding topography, its scale, and its wildlife all combine to communicate a feeling of remoteness.

Of wildlife there is much. The many loons, mergansers, herons, herring gulls, even the occasional double-crested cormorant (*Phalacrocorax auritus*), speak of an abundance of fish. The shallow waters near the three inlet channels are actively fished by the birds. The wildlife are especially attracted to the backwater, or bogan, adjacent to the north channel. At high water it becomes a fourth channel for this braided section of river. But in the summer months it is a mile-long dead-end canal. Because its entrance is well camouflaged by tall grasses and aquatic plants, animals can feed hidden and undisturbed among the reeds and alders. Dawn and dusk are active times, judging by the monotone croaks of giant bullfrogs, the dependable presence of fishing American bittern and great blue heron, the feeding of deer and moose, and the darting and swooping of insect-catching flycatchers and swallows.

The sudden howling and yipping of a pack of coyotes occasionally breaks the silence. Startling and eerie, the high-pitched chorus provides a reminder that much of what lives here is unseen. The coyote now fills the niche of the extirpated timber wolf (*Canus lupus*). Unlike the wolf, the coyote adapts to human encroachments on the wilderness and is now a permanent resident in the southern half of the boreal forest, a range once exclusively the wolf's domain.

Coyotes hunt a variety of mammals, including small rodents, snowshoe hare, beaver, and deer. They are opportunists that will also eat birds, reptiles, amphibians, fish, and insects, as well as berries and other fruits. They hunt singly, in pairs, or in packs depending on their mating and rearing

The Allagash River takes a break at Round Pond, a small body of water nestled among forested hills.

circumstances during the year. Coyotes in the eastern part of the continent are large as coyotes go. Males may weigh forty-five to fifty pounds, but this is much less than the sixty-five-to hundred-pound weights of male timber wolves.

The social order of the timber wolf is believed to be more complex than that of the coyote. Packs consist of family members and others. Wolves communicate in many ways, but most impressive to humans is their howling, which is believed to be a means of assembling the pack. Thoreau recalled a time in the 1850s when friends of his, who were moose hunting near the south end of the waterway, were serenaded by wolves: "It was a sudden burst, as if a hundred demons had broke loose,—a startling sound enough, which, if any, would make your hair stand on end, and all was still again. . . . They heard it twice only, and they said that it gave expression to the wilderness which it lacked before."[6]

The timber wolf is thought to have left Maine sometime in the middle of the nineteenth century, about the time of Thoreau's passing. However, in recent years there continue to be sporadic reports of wolves in this northern wilderness. One large wolf was reported trotting on the ice of Long Lake during the winter of 1972.[7]

Although the record is skimpy and debatable, another predator, now found only in far northern areas, may also have lived at one time in this region. This is the wolverine (*Gulo gulo*), a large, fierce weasel. Today, with the exception of the black bear, the eastern coyote is the largest remaining resident predator in the Allagash region.

Records suggest that the wolverine may have at one time inhabited northern Maine. One is pictured here on Round Pond in the lower section of the river. Today, the wolverine has retreated to the far north, along with the timber wolf.

The River to the Falls

Lew Dietz wrote that "perhaps the most beautiful section of the river is the stretch between Round Pond and Allagash Falls. . . . All along the sinuous river route solitary old-growth pines, spared by early loggers, stand like lonely sentinels, their terraced crowns rising high above the spruce canopy. Many of the spires of these ancient giants are riven by lightning strikes, the price they pay for their lordly vantage."[8]

Immediately upon leaving the quiet waters of Round Pond, the river becomes a series of whitewater rapids alternating with quiet stretches. Three miles below the pond, the river makes a sharp turn to the south. In this area a great swath of spruce-fir forest, three to four hundred yards wide and twenty miles long, was ripped away by a tornado on August 15, 1958. Tornadoes are not common in New England, but typically occur somewhere in Maine each year. Deciduous trees have now replaced the conifers in the tornado area. But beneath their broad-leaved canopies, the shade-tolerant spruce and fir wait their chance to once again exert their presence.

The river winds around a fifteen-hundred-foot mountain, one of the tallest in this area and with a trail leading to good views of the region. Beyond it the river approaches the second of its two largest tributaries, Musquacook Stream. The land is low and swampy on the south side of the approach, and large silver maples overhang the river. Though the stream drains a large area, including the five Musquacook lakes, in summer it is low and well camouflaged by the thick growth of vegetation on its banks.

A short distance up the stream from its mouth, a well-known tall dead tree once stood, supporting a spectacular osprey nest high in its top. The osprey nests over a large area of the north woods. A large, eaglelike bird, it lives near water because it eats fish almost exclusively, whereby it has earned the common name of fish hawk. The river, lakes, and streams in this region are the osprey's fishing grounds, and the nest here was in an ideal location because of the nearby Musquacook Deadwater.

The mouth of the stream marks the beginning of this deep, slow-moving, three-mile-long section of the river. Fish are plentiful here, and the osprey's whistlelike cheeping is often heard overhead. When this raptor sights a fish, it hovers, beating its large wings, then dives at high speed with its feet forward. Its black claws are long and curved, designed for grasping. Rising out of the water with its catch, the osprey will orient the body of the fish so that its head is pointed

Ospreys nest throughout the waterway and are often seen hovering over the pools and deadwaters of the river as they hunt for fish.

A white-tailed deer pauses at the edge of one of the three channels formed by the Allagash River where it enters Round Pond. These shallow channels, surrounded by lush vegetation, attract many species of wildlife in summer.

forward in order to reduce resistance when flying. Occasionally an osprey locks its talons onto a fish larger than it can handle, and, unable to release the fish, the bird drowns. One canoe party observed just such an incident here in the waterway, but in that case the osprey was able to swim and drag its prey to shore.

Ospreys are not the only birds that avail themselves of this productive deadwater. Mergansers fish here, and goldeneyes hunt the waters for aquatic insects and vegetation. While their parents search for food, goldeneye ducklings are often left on rocks, where they are almost perfectly camouflaged by the coloring of their plumage.

At the end of the deadwater the river becomes shallower and swifter. Soon it comes to the confluence of Five Fingers Brook. On the east shore of the river the brook has deposited a sandy delta that is above water in summer. The delta narrows the river at this location, and small riffles occur in the quickened water as it flows over several large rocks. The delta has created a small backwater on its upstream side, and here moose and deer frequently feed on summer evenings, sometimes together. This writer once saw a doe deer and a bull moose passing within five feet of each other while feeding in opposite directions along this shoreline.

Across the river, the high west bank feeds its gravelly, cobbly soil into the river with each high water. This bank is covered by a variety of herbaceous plants—stout goldenrod (*Solidago squarrosa*), pearly everlasting, intermediate dogbane (*Apocynum medium*), daisy fleabane (*Erigeron annuus*),

Canada hawkweed (*Hieracium canadense*), wild mint, blue vetch, blueberry, raspberry, and meadowsweet, but they do little to hold the bank in check. Speckled alder, northern white cedar, white spruce, and balsam fir are also present on the bank, but the river is strong here, and during high water the shore continues to wash away. Back in the forest beyond the river's edge, the vegetation is much less stressed, and here, beneath white spruce and fir and among thick beds of mosses, grow woodsorrel, bunchberry, and bracken fern.

Below Five Fingers Brook the river continues to widen, with accompanying shallows, gravel bars, and meandering chan-

At Five Fingers Brook, the river captures the soft hues of an evening sunset.

Approaching Allagash Falls, the river flows quietly through a floodplain of deep, fertile soils, dividing as it winds among low islands. Silver maple, American elm, balsam poplar, ostrich fern, swamp milkweed, and other plants of the northern riverine forest populate the silty banks of the river here.

nels. Islands increase in number, supporting speckled alders and a variety of shrubs and grasses. Three miles or so above Allagash Falls, the river makes a large, sweeping turn to the east, and its channel divides, becoming separated by islands. Finley Bogan comes into view on the west shore—a shallow backwater where bitterns, herons, and grebes congregate. An old beaver dam continues to hinder the entrance of Farm Brook.

McKinnon Brook also comes into the river just below the bogan. Nearby, in the spruce along the shore, Ted Janes, on his trip down the river in the late 1960s, "found the summer home of evening grosbeaks (*Hesperiphona vespertina*)."[9]

William O. Douglas also described his discoveries along the shore on his trip through this section—the "tantalizing fragrance" of sweet grass (family Gramineae), a form of field horsetail (*Equisetum* sp.), a delicate feather moss (*Hypnum* sp.), "sturdy stands" of pincushion moss (*Leucobryum glaucum*), viburnum (*Viburnum* sp.) "at deep port," thick growths of sweet gale (*Myrica gale*), sand cherry (*Prunus depressa*) heavy with fruit, rushes, bluejoint reed grass (*Calamagrostis canadensis*), needle spike sedge (perhaps *Eleocharis* sp.), Pennsylvania bitter cress (*Cardamine pensylvanica*, tall golden grass (family Gramineae), and American water willow (*Justicia americana*).[10]

NORTHERN RIVERINE FOREST

Henry Baldwin noted in his 1963 trip that above Allagash Falls "the river separated into different channels and there was a sudden change in the vegetation. Silver maple, elm, and balm-of-Gilead poplar (*Populus balsamifera* or the hybrid *x. Populus gileadensis*) grew on the islands. Red osier dogwood (*Cornus stolonifera*) and ostrich fern formed the understory. The whole had a more southern look."[11] What he saw was the northern riverine or floodplain forest.

The land above the falls is flat for three or more miles—quite like an old lake filled in with sediment. The soils are stream alluvium—silts, sands, and gravels—blanketed here during periods of high waters, usually during the spring floods. The river must work its way through its own debris; lacking guidance from knolls and hills, it has braided into several shallow channels and numerous low islands. The soils are deep and fertile but lack stability in the shifting river environment.

Those trees and other plants which survive here must be able to invade newly formed bars and lands stripped by the river's powerful floods. The silver maple is such a colonizer— a tree that competes best along riverbanks. It grows sixty to eighty feet tall, with a broad-topped, rounded crown. The undersides of the deeply and narrowly lobed leaves are silvery white, therefore its name. The American elm also grows along this floodplain, tall and imposing with its vaselike shape. In spring, flocks of purple finches are sometimes attracted to the tree when it is fruiting, and its twigs are sometimes browsed by deer.

The large balsam poplar, often called balm-of-Gilead by loggers, may grow as tall as one hundred feet here but is often shorter. The alternate, fine-toothed leaves are broadly lance shaped and pointed at the tip, often tapering somewhat at the base. Dark green and shiny above, they usually have rusty blotches on their whitish undersides. Of special interest are the fragrant, resinous buds, which are up to an inch long. In spring, after emerging from their winter's sleep, black bears have been observed feeding on these buds.

In keeping with the character of this kind of wet, fertile environment, there is a virtual tangle of plants along the river. Virgin's bower (*Clematis virginiana*) is a prevalent vine, twisting its long, purplish leafstalks around the shrubs and other vegetation. In summer its flowers are in loose clusters with creamy white, loose sepals; it has no true petals. On the waterlogged floor of this forest grow ostrich ferns (of fiddlehead epicurian fame), jewelweed (*Impatiens capensis*), sedges, turtlehead, and swamp milkweed. Animals associated with this northern riverine forest include mink, otter, spotted sandpiper, yellow warbler, wood duck, and belted kingfisher.

In spring, along the lower Allagash River, black bears are known to seek out the large, fragrant, resinous buds of the balsam poplar. Although the tree is sometimes called balm-of-Gilead by loggers, horticulturists use that name for a cultivated hybrid.

ALLAGASH FALLS

As the river approaches Allagash Falls it again narrows into one channel, and outcrops of vertically tilted gray slate begin to appear.[12] Boulders start to show up in the channel. Ahead, the rumble of the falls grows louder. The river takes a turn, and beyond rises the muffled roar of turbulent water. Closer to the falls, the river narrows and becomes swifter. The boulders are larger here and the rapids more violent.

Outcroppings of upturned slate form the lip of the falls and the gorge below. The river thunders down a major drop of twenty feet followed by a series of smaller drops. It boils and swirls furiously over deep potholes and the polished contours of the spray-filled channel—an awesome spectacle of natural beauty and power. Oriented by the ancient folds of continental collisions and zones of weakness in the upturned, thinly leaved slate, the rapids continue for over eight hundred feet, passing a small gravel beach where some of the eroded detritus of the falls is collected. All told, the river drops about thirty feet.

Even in this unstable environment many plants have gained a foothold in the dips and crevices of the bedrock that surrounds the falls—timothy (*Phleum pratense*) and other grasses, harebell (*Campanula rotundifolia*), yarrow, wild strawberry, Canada goldenrod (*Solidago canadensis*), hairy goldenrod (*Solidago hispida*), red-osier dogwood, meadow rue, ostrich fern, fireweed, and blue vetch. Virgin's bower and Virginia creeper (*Parthenocissus quinquefolia*) are tangled among the alders and other shrubs. Sphagnum mosses inhabit the wetter areas, and fern mosses cover wet, shaded, vertical surfaces of the slate rock. Out on the open rocks, large patches of green map lichen (*Rhizocarpon geographicum*) add a dimension of color and interest. Apple moss (*Bartramia pomiformis*) is also found here. Northern white cedar, balsam fir, and balsam poplar grow higher up above the rocks. One has the impression that the river is more alive here than at any other location.

The river narrows and roars to life at Allagash Falls as it thunders down over nearly vertical beds of slate into a dark-walled pool thirty feet below.

Final Run

In its final fourteen miles, from the falls to its confluence with the St. John, the river continues fresh and fast. Rapids are frequent and often long. Slate ledges interrupt the boulder-strewn riverbed—a reminder of the falls above. The slope of the river is readily apparent, creating a sensation of looking down an inclined plane, accompanied by the expectation of a current faster than it is. The river widens, and by midsummer the pronounced meandering of its channels among the numerous rocks and gravel bars is more readily visible. Islands appear, often populated by silver maple. Most of the islands support a dense covering of grasses that attract deer. Along the shoreline, white birches become increasingly noticeable.

A little more than a mile below the falls, McKeen Brook enters on the east side. During the spring breakup, ice has been known to back up to the falls from here. Less than a mile beyond, Big Brook comes in through its forested corridor. Below this confluence of brook and river is a large pool where ospreys fish. Herons and ducks also are seen here. For the next two miles, the river runs adjacent to banks on its east shore that were formed by ancient streams running along the edge of a stagnant glacier. A ridge of glacial debris follows—an end moraine deposited at the glacier's melting edge.

Eight miles below the falls, the Seboomook Slate makes its last major show, and Twin Brook Rapids dips and turns north. At the base of the rapids a large slate outcrop rises on the west shore. The lower portion of the outcrop near the river is highly scoured, smoothly contoured, and potholed. At higher levels on the ledges the vertically fissured calcareous slate helps to provide mineral nutrients that, along with the cool temperature and moisture, produce the proper environment required by the New England violet (*Viola nova-angliae*).

Around the first of June the ledges' deep vertical cracks are sprinkled with reddish-violet blossoms of a rather rare violet, known only from a few locations in the northeast.[13] The blossoms of bird's-eye primrose (*Primula mistassinica*), so-called because of the yellow eye centered in its pink or pale purple

The rare bird's-eye primrose finds a foothold in a fissure in Twin Brook Ledges.

The Allagash Wilderness Waterway ends officially at Twin Brook
Ledges, eight miles below Allagash Falls. A boulder, worn smooth by
the river's jostling, sitting high and dry on the ledges, is evidence of
the river's fluctuating levels.

flower, provide company for the violet. This boreal plant reaches its southern limit in northern New England. The ledges have captured enough soil and nutrients to support other plants too, including tussocks of sedges of the *Scirpus* and *carex* genera; the sun-loving wild strawberry; early meadow parsnip, or golden Alexander (*Zizia aurea*), with its wheel-like umbel of bright yellow flowers; wild chive (*Allium schoeno-prasum* var. *sibiricum*) with its strong odor suggestive of onions; and dwarf sand cherry (*Prunus depressa*) and starry false Solomon's seal (*Smilacina stellata*) with their delicate white flowers. Swamp buttercup (*Ranunculus septentrionalis*), sporting its glossy yellow blossoms, grows behind the ledges near the riverbank.

The last six miles of the river continue through the mixture of hardwoods and spruce and fir that characterize this northern forest. In autumn the ridges and hills blaze with the colors of the hardwoods contrasting with the dark greens of the conifers. Beaver are in evidence, taking advantage of the nutritious inner bark of the deciduous trees close to the river.

Finally the river flows out of the forest, still youthful, clear, and fresh. With a magnificent S-shaped flourish, it makes a rocky dash to the St. John. There, mingling with the islands of that broad river, it loses its identity and disappears as quietly as it began some hundred miles upstream, secluded among remote springs and seeps, shaded by spruce and fir.

The Allagash River sweeps over one last set of rapids, then flows quietly again as it joins the St. John. Here, a clump of red osier dogwood flowers near the river's mouth.

This is the Allagash, a fragile strip of waterway symbolizing the value of America's diminishing wilderness. It challenges us to not only protect our wild rivers but to approach the future with a humbler attitude toward the natural world to which we are connected—like a river to the land.

"Red in the morning." The Allagash River at Five Fingers Brook. One of America's wild and scenic rivers, the Allagash epitomizes our diminishing wilderness.

Chapter Notes

PREFACE

1. Justice William O. Douglas, one of the early proponents for the preservation of the Allagash, wrote eloquently of the waterway in his book *My Wilderness: East of Katahdin* (Garden City, N.Y.: Doubleday & Co., 1961), 244.

THE HEADWATERS

1. Many details of the waterway's glacial history appearing throughout the book were derived from J. Steven Kite, Thomas V. Lowell, and Woodrow B. Thompson, eds., *Contributions to the Quaternary Geology of Northern Maine and Adjacent Canada,* Bulletin 37 (Augusta, Maine: Maine Geological Survey, Department of Conservation, 1988). Information was also obtained from Woodrow B. Thompson and Harold W. Borns, Jr., eds., *Surficial Geology Map of Maine* (Augusta, Maine: Maine Geological Survey, Department of Conservation, 1985).

2. The dimensions of the watershed described are the original measurements when the drainage from the headwaters and some of the large lakes flowed north down the Allagash River. In 1842 most of the water from Allagash, Chamberlain, and Telos lakes was diverted south into the Penobscot watershed through a canal built at the end of Telos Lake. Today only a relatively small amount of water from these lakes still flows north, going by way of Lock Dam on Chamberlain Lake.

3. Henry D. Thoreau, *The Maine Woods* (New York: Thomas Y. Crowell & Co., 1906), 301.

4. An encounter with a Canada lynx by Milford Kidney at Lock Dam on Chamberlain Lake was described by Dorothy Kidney in her book *A Home in the Wilderness* (New York: A.S. Barnes & Co., 1976), 72–73.

5. Ezekiel Holmes and C.H. Hitchcock, *Second Annual Report upon the Natural History and Geology of the State of Maine* (Augusta, Maine: Stevens & Sayward, 1862), 352.

6. George S. Kephart, *Campfires Rekindled* (Marion, Mass.: Channing Books, 1977), 3.

7. Ibid., 2–3.

8. The narrative describing the character and origin of the bedrock geology of the Allagash Lake area drew heavily on Stephen G. Pollock's map, *Bedrock Geology of the Caucomgomoc Lake Area, Maine* (Augusta, Maine: Maine Geological Survey, Department of Conservation, 1985) and on conversations with him regarding theories of formation.

THE LARGE LAKES

1. Much of the description of the lake region's bedrock geology, including fossils, draws upon Bradford A. Hall, *Stratigraphy of the Southern End of the Munsungun Anticlinorium, Maine,* Bulletin 22 (Augusta, Maine: Maine Geological Survey and Department of Economic Development, 1970). Additional information about the bedrock geology of the entire waterway region was derived from Philip H. Osberg, Arthur M. Hussey II, and Gary M. Boone, eds., *Bedrock Geologic Map of Maine* (Augusta, Maine: Maine Geological Survey, Department of Conservation, 1985).

2. Information on postglacial, prehistoric wildlife came from Arthur Spiess, "Comings and Goings: Maine's Prehistoric Wildlife," *Habitat: Journal of the Maine Audubon Society,* 5 (January 1988): 30–33.

3. Details on the revegetation of the region following the last glacier drew heavily on the article by George L. Jacobson, Jr., and Ronald B. Davis, "Temporary and Transitional: The Real Forest Primeval—The Evolution of Maine's Forests Over 14,000 Years," *Habitat: Journal of the Maine Audubon Society,* 5 (January 1988): 27–29.

4. Information on the region's soils came from the soil interpretation record sheets published by the United States Department of Agriculture, Soil Conservation Service.

5. Dorothy Boone Kidney, *Away from It All* (New York: A.S. Barnes & Co., 1969), 181.

6. Henry D. Thoreau, *The Maine Woods* (New York: Thomas Y. Crowell & Co., 1906), 259. Note: scientific names were added by the author.

7. Ibid., 244–45.

8. Thomas Sedgwick Steele, *Paddle and Portage* (Boston: Estes and Lauriat, 1882), 46.

9. Lew Dietz, *The Allagash* (New York: Holt, Rinehart & Winston, 1968), 78.

10. Information on the last caribou legally killed in Maine came from the "Maine Talgia" column in *The Maine Sportsman* (January 1990): 9.

11. A detailed overview of freshwater wetland communities, including bogs and fens, is contained in the book by Dean Bennett, *Maine's Natural Heritage* (Camden, Maine: Down East Books, 1988), 98–119.

12. Much of the description of Chamberlain Fen was based on the unpublished report by Eric Sorenson and Naomi Edelson, *Chamberlain Fen* (Augusta, Maine: Critical Areas Program, Maine State Planning Office, June 3, 1987).

13. *Pertica quadrifaria* is described in a report by its discoverers, Andrew E. Kasper, Jr., and Henry N. Andrews, Jr., "Pertica : A New Genus of Devonian Plants from Northern Maine," *American Journal of Botany*, 59 (October 1972): 897–911.

14. Some of the description of the Eagle Lake old-growth forest came from the unpublished report *Eagle Lake Old-growth Pine Stand* (Augusta, Maine: Critical Areas Program, Maine State Planning Office, September 20, 1978).

15. Information on the old-growth forest near Soper Brook came from the report *Ziegler Campground Old Growth White Pine Stand* (Augusta, Maine: Critical Areas Program, Maine State Planning Office, June 1979).

16. Steele, *Paddle and Portage*, 53.

17. Thoreau, *The Maine Woods*, 261.

18. Helen Hamlin, *Nine Mile Bridge* (New York: W.W. Norton & Co., 1945), 126–127.

19. William O. Douglas, *My Wilderness: East of Katahdin* (Garden City, N.Y.: Doubleday & Co., 1961), 251–52. Note: scientific names were added by the author.

20. Hamlin, *Nine Mile Bridge*, 75.

21. Dorothy Boone Kidney, *Wilderness Journal* (Portland, Maine: Guy Gannett Publishing Co., 1980), 60–107.

THE RIVER

1. "Maine Talgia," *The Maine Sportsman* (January 1990): 9.

2. The wildlife drama involving the deer and coyote was witnessed by the author and his wife on March 6, 1992, while photographing the rapids.

3. Henry I. Baldwin, "Skyline Sketches: Allagash, Briefly Visited," *Appalachia* (1963): 82.

4. Annette Jackson, *My Life in the Maine Woods* (New York: W.W. Norton & Co., 1954), 48–49.

5. William O. Douglas, *My Wilderness: East of Katahdin* (Garden City, N.Y.: Doubleday & Co., 1961), 261–62. Note: scientific names were added by the author.

6. Henry D. Thoreau, *The Maine Woods* (New York: Thomas Y. Crowell & Co., 1906), 245.

7. Personal communication from Jim Drake, longtime resident of the Allagash wilderness.

8. Lew Dietz, *The Allagash* (New York: Holt, Rinehart and Winston, 1968), xx.

9. Ted Janes, "Wilderness Trout Trip—The Allagash Story," *Outdoor Life* (August 1964): 59. Note: scientific names were added by the author.

10. Douglas, *My Wilderness: East of Katahdin*, 241–43. Note: scientific names were added by the author.

11. Baldwin, "Skyline Sketches: Allagash, Briefly Visited," 83. Note: scientific name was added by the author.

12. Allagash Falls is also described in the unpublished report *Allagash Falls* (Augusta, Maine: Critical Areas Program, Maine State Planning Office, June 11, 1979).

13. Information on the rare plants at Twin Brook Ledges is contained in the unpublished report by Susan C. Gawler, *Allagash Ledges Rare Violet Station* (Augusta, Maine: Critical Areas Program, Maine State Planning Office, February 1982).

PHOTOGRAPH NOTES

All photographs were made with Nikon FE2 bodies, of which three were often carried in the field. Nikkor lenses were used and included 18mm, 24mm, 50mm, 105mm and 200mm micro, and 400mm f3.5 IF ED. The 400mm lens was chosen because it is one of the longest telephotos that allows taking hand-held wildlife photographs from a canoe. With Kodachrome 64 film, its widest apertures enabled photographs to be taken at 1/500 second or 1/1000 second. A motor drive was frequently used with this lens and occasionally a 1.4X tele-extender.

Most work utilized a tripod with quick release plates. Filters were rarely used, but on special occasions polarizing, warming, and neutral density filters were employed. Extreme closeups were taken with a combination of micro lenses and extension tubes, sometimes in conjunction with reversed lenses. Photographs taken underwater, at water level in rapids, and at waterfalls required the use of an underwater housing.

Flash equipment consisted of a Nikon SB-16, two SB-18s, and special high-speed equipment for some birds and insects. The high-speed flash photographs were taken at 1/20,000 and 1/33,000 of a second and also incorporated the use of triggering devices with light beams.

Fujichrome Velvia 50 film was chosen to photograph most landscapes and wildflowers because of its saturated colors. Kodachrome 64 was the choice film for most wildlife. These fine-grained films were also selected for their sharpness, which, with a few exceptions, was a sought-after attribute. Other factors assisting in obtaining sharp images included locking up the mirror, utilizing a cable release, using fast shutter speeds and middle-range f-stops, checking depth-of-field, and focusing at the hyperfocal distance.

Beyond considerations of equipment, choice of film, and technique, nature photography requires a combination of planning and visualizing images that convey a concept or feeling, putting oneself in a position where there is a likelihood of having desired photographic opportunities, being prepared for the unexpected, and luck. Patience, good humor, and a positive perspective fill the long gaps between successes. But, like finding the right word to convey a feeling, the capture of even one interesting subject—properly exposed, sharp, and well composed—among three dozen newly processed transparencies can bring its own special brand of creative pleasure and satisfaction.

Index

Page numbers in **boldface** refer to illustrations or photographs. Scientific names for plants and animals will be found on the first page referenced for each.